Richard Cottingham:

The True Story of The Torso Killer

by Jack Rosewood

**Historical Serial Killers and Murderers
True Crime by Evil Killers
Volume 20**

Copyright © 2016 by Wiq Media

ALL RIGHTS RESERVED

No part of this book may be reproduced, stored in a retrieval system, or transmitted in any form or by any means, electronic, mechanical, photocopying, recording, scanning, or otherwise, without the prior written permission of the publisher.

DISCLAIMER:

This serial killer biography includes quotes from those closely involved in the case of American serial killer Richard Cottingham, also known as the Torso Killer, and it is not the author's intention to defame or intentionally hurt anyone involved. The interpretation of the events leading up to Cottingham's arrest and capture are the author's as a result of researching the serial killer's story from a variety of different sources including newspaper stories and interviews, televised interviews and documentaries about the case. Any comments made about the psychopathic, narcissistic or sadistic behavior of Cottingham – one of the most deranged murderers to prowl Times Square - are the sole opinion and responsibility of the person quoted.

Free Bonus!

Get two free books when you sign up to my VIP newsletter at www.jackrosewood.com

150 interesting trivia about serial killers and the story of serial killer Herbert Mullin.

Contents

Introduction 1

CHAPTER 1: A murderer is born 3

    The making of a paraphilia 6

    Tales of a dark side 8

    More, more, more 9

    The calling card is like a fingerprint 10

    The meaningless of others 11

    Evil hiding behind a normal life 12

CHAPTER 2: Murder on his mind 14

    A gruesome discovery 15

    An unlikely suspect 16

    At work, Cottingham talks a big talk 17

CHAPTER 3: Would a wife mean a new life? 21

    Setting off for a fresh start 23

    He had a way about him 23

    A madman hiding in plain sight 25

CHAPTER 4: Woman's disappearance triggers concern 27

Mary Ann's horrifying last hours 28

Cottingham flies under the radar, but only for a while 30

The chase begins 31

Another woman survives torturous night with Cottingham 33

Police again make horrific find 34

CHAPTER 5: Prostitutes made for easy prey 36

Midwestern girls were particularly vulnerable 37

Sex workers at high risk for murder 38

CHAPTER 6: The torture killer 41

The games sadists play 42

Empathy? Surprisingly yes, say two experts 43

Don't get it twisted. Empathy and sympathy are not the same 45

CHAPTER 7: A murder that became unforgettable 47

Torture becomes a sick game 48

All fun and games 50

Hiding evidence in plain sight 51

Firefighters arrive to find unspeakable horror 52

- The Times Square Ripper revealed? 53
- Escalating depravity a common trait 54

CHAPTER 8: A return to hotel hell 56
- Evidence begins to add up 58
- Time between crimes escalates 60
- A gruesome second fire 60
- Fingerprints, photos lead to victim's identification 62
- Trouble in 'paradise' 63

CHAPTER 9: Leslie Ann O'Dell suffers to save countless victims 65
- Hope, rising 66
- Luck for Cottingham finally runs out 70
- Cottingham had gotten careless 71
- The great escape foiled 72

CHAPTER 10: The interrogation 74
- Attempted murder called consensual 75
- Questioning goes cold 78
- A treasure trove of trophies 78
- Souvenirs of death 79
- Charges pile up quickly 81

Cottingham was all the buzz at Blue Cross Blue Shield 83

CHAPTER 11: Cottingham on trial 86

A surprising suspect 87

Chilling since childhood 89

The timeline of Valerie Ann Street's death 91

Girlfriend talks 92

Survivors' testimony leaves courtroom reeling 92

Prosecution takes on psychopath 94

An inside look 95

Cottingham goes on trial for murder of Mary Ann Carr 97

Mary Ann Carr trial beings again 98

Curses, escape attempt foiled again 100

CHAPTER 12: New York trial 102

CHAPTER 13: Cottingham confesses to first murder, solving cold case 104

Other cold cases could have been Cottingham 105

CHAPTER 14: The Aftermath 107

Two books are born 107

Sitting down with danger 109

A fascination with danger 111

Face to face with a madman 112

Like Santa, but with a sadistic side 112

Cottingham doesn't wonder 'why me' 114

Communal with madness a way to solve
unanswered questions 116

Question of 'why' will never have answers 119

More books by Jack Rosewood 125

GET THESE BOOKS FOR FREE 1

A Note From The Author 131

Introduction

His sadistic side made sex-crazed serial killer Richard Cottingham notorious from the start.

"It was a very big story because of how gruesome it was," said New Jersey resident Richard Neumann, who ran high school track with Cottingham, a sexual sadist whose desires were fueled by the pain he inflicted on women he thought were his for the taking.

Arrested for the murders of five women although he has admitted to killing almost 100, Cottingham has never expressed a shred of remorse for the torture he forced his victims to endure or the pain he brought to the families of the women whose lives he took, robbing them of years of memories.

In fact, he expressed nothing at all.

"No feeling," he said to Canadian journalist Nadia Fezzani, who in 2011 snagged the only interview Cottingham ever gave aside from police interrogations. "Nothing. I forgot. Like it didn't happen. I could put myself into a zone to do something like that."

In the media, he became known as the Torso Killer for the gruesome dismemberments of his victims' bodies, conducted as his crime scenes escalated and he required more and more deviant behavior in order to satisfy his sexual urges.

A psychopath with little regard for human life, Cottingham was one of those guys who was truly born to kill.

"A psychopath already starts at a disadvantage," said forensic psychologist Katherine Ramsland. "And as he then gets exposed to things that lure him into wanting power over other people, the idea of being born to kill comes pretty close to him."

And it was just a matter of time until his proclivity for pornography, prostitutes, and S&M led him to take a step into a dark side that coworkers and his devoted family never expected.

But then, they didn't really know him all that well.

They just thought they did.

CHAPTER 1:
A murderer is born

Richard Cottingham was born on November 25, 1946, in the Bronx, New York.

Harry S. Truman was president, the Vincente Minelli movie "Undercurrent" starring Katharine Hepburn, Robert Taylor and Robert Mitchum was playing at theaters and the songs listeners heard most on the radio were the two tunes topping the charts, Hoagy Carmichael's "Huggin' and Chalkin'" and "It's All Over Now" by Peggy Lee.

His was a typical New York childhood, although he was lonely when he was away from home, as he had trouble making friends with his classmates and was considered a bit of an odd boy out.

That's the thing with psychopaths, though. While manipulative and charming, they have little regard for others, so they have trouble forming genuine relationships. When they do, they are superficial at best, and the psychopath feels completely superior to the others around him.

When Cottingham was 12 years old and in the seventh grade, his family moved to River Vale, New Jersey, a small township in Bergen County that was an idyllic location to grow up. (It remains so. In a 2007 survey appearing in Money magazine, it was ranked number 29 on the list of 100 Best Places to Live.)

Again, his was a normal middle-class household. His father worked in insurance, and his mother was a homemaker who, according to Trumann, doted on her son and his two younger siblings.

They lived in a large split-level house with plenty of space for three kids on Cleveland Avenue in River Vale.

"It was a great area to grow up in," said Neumann. "There were plenty of parks, open space."

And his was a family full of love, Neumann added.

"I know his mother was devoted to him," Cottingham's former classmate said.

Cottingham attended St. Andrews, a co-ed parochial school, but continued to struggle with establishing friendships, so instead of hanging out with his classmates, after school he spent time at home, where he had a hobby raising homing pigeons.

The solitary activity suited him, and it kept him from dwelling on his loneliness at school.

It wasn't until he enrolled at Pascack Valley High School that he finally made a few friends.

"I met Richard on the athletic field," said Neumann, who was numb with horror after learning that the classmate who'd lived just two streets away from him had taken the lives of at least five women. "Richard stood apart in that he wasn't always at practice, he wasn't a joiner, he didn't have a nickname, and he wasn't part of our little clique. He had kind of a wise guy attitude about him. I don't think he was crazy about authority, I believe."

Cottingham did have a group of three friends, Neumann said, and in that group, Cottingham stood out as the clear leader.

Again, that would be normal for a psychopath with grandiose ideas about themselves that usually lean toward narcissism. It's just that others never really saw him in the same light.

"There was really nothing extraordinary about him, except that he was kind of removed from the mainstream," another classmate said in an interview with the Record, a newspaper based in Bergen County, New Jersey that covered the Cottingham case extensively.

Although Neumann remembered Cottingham being attracted to women, he didn't remember him ever having a girlfriend.

"When he spoke about women, it was kind of in a negative way," Neumann said. "I certainly remember him talking among his friends and perhaps in gym class about what girls attracted him."

Cottingham, it seems, liked a certain type of woman.

"He would talk about the girls in class or the girls out on the street who were better endowed, larger breasted. That just sort of seemed to be a key attraction for him," his former classmate remembered.

While most guys have preferences like Cottingham's (there aren't numerous porn magazines and websites devoted to girls with big boobs for nothing), most will say, "I'm a breast man" or "I'm all about the booty," but won't take it further than that.

In Cottingham's case, those large breasts he coveted would eventually become fetishized, a paraphilia necessary for arousal, and the women he encountered who had the look he liked would suffer for it. And so would their breasts, which Cottingham bit like a calling card, leaving a lasting mark of his depraved nature for the women who survived.

The making of a paraphilia

Psychologists describe paraphilia as abnormal sexual desires that may include extreme According to experts, paraphilias can include fetishes, such as Cottingham's penchant for large breasts, exhibitionism, pedophilia, frotteurism (the desire to rub one's genitalia against a non-consenting person such as someone on a crowded subway, for example), transvestitism (the desire to wear women's clothing), voyeurism, sexual masochism (the desire to be humiliated, abused or subjugated during sexual activity as a way to achieve sexual excitement) and sadism (the desire to inflict pain or injury on another in order to be aroused).

or dangerous activities.

While some are perfectly harmless, others, such as frotteurism, sadism or necrophilia, for example, can be illegal or deadly.

"In most cases, the individual with a paraphilia has difficulty developing personal and sexual relationships with others," say the experts at WebMD.com, who added that most paraphilias turn up during the teen years, and can last into adulthood, often diminishing over time.

Men are 20 times more likely than women to develop a paraphilia, and although experts are not certain how they develop, most people can live normal lives, saving their paraphilic desires for either fantasies to accompany masturbation sessions or as part of mutually satisfying sex with a partner.

For the dark, demented, and evil side of paraphilia, however, fetishes and desires often show themselves at a very early age, and rarely diminish, but instead bubble beneath the surface until erupting in a blood-soaked burst of violence.

Cottingham, for example, had two forms of paraphilia, his fetish for large breasts and his desire for sadistic sex that continued to escalate. He did not share his fetishes with a partner, but instead initially satisfied his urges with fantasy, until those fantasies were no longer sexually satisfying for him.

He was then forced to bring his fantasies demonically to life through a series of savage murders that only grew more and more diabolical in nature.

Eventually, Cottingham's list of fetishes, each one more cruel and barbaric than the one before, would lead to crime scenes that left even the most hardened police detectives and other law enforcement officials nearly speechless.

"These were very bizarre and bloody crimes," said Bergen County District Attorney Dennis Calo. "Beheadings, burnt, chopped up."

For Cottingham, it was nothing more than a game he played, albeit with completely unwilling partners.

Tales of a dark side

"These individuals hare very dark and perverse sexual fantasies from very early on," said forensic psychologist Louis Schlesinger, an expert in the field of serial killers. "Usually, 10 to 20 years before any real activities take place, fantasies are born."

Cottingham eventually blamed his own sexual sadism on pornography, which often starts with a Playboy magazine hidden beneath a mattress and evolves into other forms.

More, more, more

"It's a common trajectory with sadistic sexual serial murderers," said Ramsland, who said that their fantasies can be inspired by something as simple as a catalogue of women in their underwear – think the Victoria's Secret and Frederick's of Hollywood circulars that once arrived in many a mailbox – and continue to grow as they require more and more stimulation to reach the same levels of arousal.

Part of that need for more stimulation stems from the way sexual serial killers fantasize.

According to the FBI's Behavioral Science Unit, many sexual serial killers obsess over their fantasies, spending more and more time preoccupied with the fantasy, which becomes more detailed with passing time.

"Many serial killers have confessed to a morbid preoccupation with fantasy during childhood," said Scott A. Bonn Ph.D., in an article appearing in Psychology Today. "For example, Ed Kemper, the 'Co-ed Killer,' who was severely abused as a child by his mother, has said, 'I knew long before I started killing that I was going to be killing; that it was going to end up like that.

The fantasies were too strong. They were going on for too long and were too elaborate.'"

Add masturbation to the mix, and the fantasies, which in Cottingham's case included images of himself torturing women who were at his mercy, become mingled with the sexual desires of the sexual serial killer, and they in almost all cases grow more and more intense.

The calling card is like a fingerprint

Just as important as the compulsion to bring the fantasy to life is the element or elements that are unique to a particular murderer, experts say.

"As a person dreams and thinks of his fantasies over time, he develops a need to express those fantasies. Most serial killers have been living with their fantasies for years before they finally bubble to the surface," according to Robert Keppel in the book "Signature Killers," an exploration into why serial sexual murderers develop personalized elements that are present at every crime scene, as important as a signature on a piece of art.

For Cottingham, the most common signature was savage bite marks on the breasts of his victims, which became more horrific with each incident.

"Others want more, and if that is what arouses them, they will continue to get more extreme," said Ramsland. "Not all serial killers are sadistic sexual murderers. Those who are tend to become very extreme with what they do to their victims."

Cottingham went over the edge.

The meaningless of others

A man who also was gifted with the tendencies of a narcissist who felt he was above the world, Cottingham believed that his needs trumped those of others, so he had no trouble seeing his victims as little more than toys put on earth solely to fulfill his own sadistic desires.

"It's common for narcissists to believe they're better than others, and obviously at heart they're insecure," Ramsland said. "But he just has distain for what other people are doing and doesn't really want to be invested in it. He thinks he's superior to everybody else."

Narcissists don't take responsibility for their actions and refuse to admit that they have faults or are ever at fault, even if they go on a years-long murder spree.

Cottingham refused to plead guilty, despite the overwhelming amount of extremely incriminating evidence that was found when he was caught, and he made a point of blaming his victims, years after his arrest. They were in the wrong place at the wrong time, he said, and that was not on him.

Evil hiding behind a normal life

In his senior high school pictures, Cottingham wore slicked back hair and a nice suit. There was no smile on his face or in his eyes, but to those around him he didn't seem unlike any of the other guys graduating as a member of the class of 1964, with the Beatles as background music to the early days of both the Vietnam War and the civil rights movement.

After graduating from high school, Cottingham went to work as a computer operator at his father's insurance company, Metropolitan Life, which for years used Charlie Brown, Snoopy, and the rest of the "Peanuts" gang to sell life insurance.

Seemingly innocuous, Cottingham used his nondescript work as a shield of sorts, and he melted into the business casual atmosphere of insurance.

While at Met Life, Cottingham beefed up his resume by taking as many computer classes as he could, and after two years he moved on to Blue Cross Blue Shield of Greater New York.

"He worked in midtown Manhattan in the heart of the business district, at Blue Cross Blue Shield, which is a very substantial insurance company," said Donald Conway, who would eventually serve as Cottingham's defense attorney at the first of his four trials.

At Blue Cross Blue Shield, he shared a work station with Dominick Volpe.

The two worked the 3 to 11 p.m. shift, which left mornings and nights free for Cottingham to feed his fantasies, hanging out at S&M clubs, learning the fine art of domination.

"I and Richard worked on a console together, chatting a lot," Volpe said. "He was well-read, up to date on current events. He was pretty smart."

He was also living a double life and was a Jekyll and Hyde beyond anything Volpe or anyone else in Cottingham's inner circle had ever imagined.

CHAPTER 2:
Murder on his mind

A year into the job at Blue Cross Blue Shield, Cottingham murdered Nancy Schiava Vogel, who was somehow sidetracked on her way to play bingo at her neighborhood church.

It was on Friday, October 27, 1967, and 29-year-old Nancy told her husband of nine years, Henry, that she was going out to play bingo at St. Margaret Roman Catholic Church in Little Ferry, New Jersey.

Henry wasn't worried because bingo was a regular tradition in the predominantly Italian Catholic neighborhood. But when the late-night news was over and Nancy still wasn't home, he started to worry.

And when the mother of two still hadn't returned home by the next day, which was totally out of character for the loving mom, a frantic Henry reported her missing.

Police launched a search but turned up nothing in or around the neighborhood suggesting anything had happened.

A gruesome discovery

On Monday, however, two 12-year-old girls had just gotten home from school at St. Francis Parochial and were in the upstairs bedroom of one of the girls when they noticed what looked like a waxy mannequin in a car on the street below.

They went to investigate, and after looking inside the vehicle and seeing that it wasn't a mannequin after all, ran to the house of a neighbor, who summoned police.

The 1960 four-door Rambler Nancy had been driving was parked on Homestead Place near a neighborhood park. Inside the car, police found the missing housewife, beaten and strangled. She was naked and her hands were tied in front of her, bound with a thin nylon cord.

Her clothes were folded neatly and placed beneath her body.

Nancy had apparently never made it to the bingo game. Packages from Valley Fair Mall in the trunk of the car containing two pairs of shoes and a blouse suggested that she had been sidetracked by the lure of shopping, and police now believed that someone she met at the mall likely had something to do with her murder, and they began to seek out witnesses.

At the crime scene, evidence showed that Nancy had fought hard for her life. Her face was bruised, and there were signs of a serious struggle.

Still, a rope or tie around her neck had led to her death from asphyxiation, according to the coroner's report, and that was a fight she had not been able to win.

Police centered their investigation on those who knew Nancy, including the friend she had planned to meet at bingo.

That friend confirmed that Nancy had never turned up at the church.

Other leads, including a man's recollection that he'd seen Nancy talking to two men, one of them he described as a hippie, never panned out.

A week after her body was found slumped over in her car, Nancy's case went cold, and her family was left with questions they feared would never be answered.

An unlikely suspect

Cottingham was not yet 21 the year he killed Nancy Vogel.

The two both lived in Little Ferry, New Jersey, and Nancy likely thought little of it when Cottingham approached her car after running into her at the mall. It might have been easy to talk her into driving somewhere other than bingo, given his silver-tongued approach to attracting his victims.

"He had known Mrs. Vogel," said Bergen County Prosecutor John Molinelli. "They were not strangers. He lived in Little Ferry, Mrs. Vogel lived in Little Ferry. So they did know each other."

While the particulars of the encounter aren't known, Nancy was killed in her car, which Cottingham then drove to a different location in order to prevent her from being found for a while.

"He did murder her in the vehicle and then park the vehicle," Molinelli said.

At the time, there was nothing about him that would make him appear to be a suspect, unless police were listening in on his conversations at work.

At work, Cottingham talks a big talk

At the console he shared with Dominick Volpe, Cottingham didn't edit himself when he chatted with his coworker.

"He talked about crazy things, but we never thought he would do crazy things," Volpe said. "I get chills on my arms thinking about it now, 35 years later. It was a shock.

"He was very upfront about it, bragging about prostitutes, S&M, gambling, all the vices that he had he bragged about," Volpe added. "He liked the slave thing, the handcuffs…"

Essentially, he took pleasure in having control over others, and that, combined with Cottingham's love of living on the edge, made his an ideal candidate for murder.

"He was a gambler, and he was not afraid to take chances on anything," said Volpe. "He would always win, usually. He always said he could get out of anything. He used that gambling thing for everything that he did. He was a winner."

Or so he bragged, anyway.

And while it would be more than 40 years before Cottingham would be connected to the murder of Nancy Vogel and forced to pay the price, eventually, that winning streak would come to an end.

It's a surprise that his fall from grace didn't come sooner, giving his favorite topics of conversation with the guys he hung around with at work.

"He was strange. Most of the stuff we would talk about, he'd talk about what he did after work," Volpe said. "He'd talk about S&M clubs he'd go to, he talked about prostitutes. He used to talk about how he could lure prostitutes out of Manhattan, and he always had two pocketfuls of cash, thousands of dollars. He would show prostitutes cash and take them to New Jersey."

Still, stories of S&M clubs with bondage equipment, whips, and ball gags could have been just big talk from the guy sitting next to him at the console, Volpe thought.

"When you're talking at work, some of it you take with a grain of salt. It goes one ear and out the other," he said.

But the narcissist in Cottingham felt so untouchable that he talked a totally truthful game at work about his nighttime escapades, and was not one bit shy about sharing his dangerous BDSM activities with his coworkers.

Because he had more on his mind than sex, however, Cottingham felt more at home in his own New Jersey stomping grounds, where he knew the territory and the locations that were safest for him to carry out his crimes. Those flashes of cash were an easy draw for the desperate whores working Times Square and allowed him to entice them to places where he himself felt safer.

As he told Nadia Fezzani, after it was over, it was if nothing had happened, and he erased it from his memory, except for the times he fantasized about bigger and better murder scenes.

But even if his mind was able to put aside his crimes, his body sometimes gave him away.

"The thing I remember most about him is that he couldn't sit still," said Volpe. "He would be sitting in his office chair shaking, his legs were shaking, his back was shaking, and he would keep that up for a whole shift, for eight, nine hours straight."

With an off-hours life like that of Richard Cottingham, anyone would be a bit jittery.

It would also appear that Cottingham drank to quiet the demons raging inside him and keep his nerves in check.

In 1969, he was arrested for drunk driving, an offense that earned him 10 days in jail and a $50 fine.

CHAPTER 3:
Would a wife mean a new life?

On May 3, 1970, Cottingham married his wife, Janet, a pretty woman with long, thick, dark hair and the large breasts Cottingham favored, at Our Lady of Lourdes Church in Queens Village, New York.

The church was Roman Catholic and made of stone, suggesting strength that neither 23-year-old Cottingham nor his marriage would ever possess.

And as for any trouble the new couple would someday have, for now, fuggedaboutit, as the Italians in his New Jersey neighborhood might have said.

Cottingham and Janet moved into a cute little apartment at Ledgewood Terrace in Little Ferry, a borough in Bergen County, New Jersey, that's likely today most famous for being the birthplace of "Cake Boss" baker Buddy Valastro.

The move allowed the couple to live a safe, suburban lifestyle while he commuted to work in NYC, via one of two New Jersey Public Transport buses with lines that provided transportation to mid-town Manhattan.

Of course, there were a few blips in their happy little marriage.

On August 21, 1972, Cottingham was arrested and convicted of shoplifting at Stern's Department Store in nearby Paramus, New Jersey. Again, he was ordered to pay a $50 fine.

Plus, there were affairs. Apparently Cottingham's sexual urges weren't completely satisfied by his wife, who might not have been into the bondage and discipline fantasies he'd had since he was young, or by the prostitutes he bragged about picking up to his co-workers. He was, it seemed, always wanting more.

On September 4, 1973, about a month before his first child was born, he was arrested on robbery, assault, and sodomy charges, although those charges were ultimately dropped.

For many women it would have been enough to bring the marriage to an end, but Janet toughed it out, perhaps believing the stories her husband told her about how it wasn't him, the police were wrong, it was all a terrible mistake. It was never his fault, after all.

Their oldest son, Blair, was born on October 15, 1973, and it should have been a happy time for Richard and Janet Cottingham.

But Cottingham, it seems, couldn't manage to stay out of trouble.

A few months after the boy's birth, Cottingham was charged with unlawful imprisonment and robbery, but again, the case was dismissed.

Setting off for a fresh start

In 1975, likely as a way to give his family a new start after creating what was likely significant family stress over his arrest record, Cottingham moved them to a three-bedroom rental home at 29 Vreeland St., in Lodi, New Jersey, a place that currently rents for almost $2,500 a month.

That same year, the Cottinghams greeted their second son, Scott, on March 28, 1975. Their only daughter, Jenny, followed soon after, on October 13, 1976.

Between the births of his two children, Cottingham laid low, but that wasn't going to last for long.   .

He had a way about him

Soon after their last child was born, Cottingham began an extra marital affair with a woman named Barbara Lucas. The relationship lasted for two years, ending in 1980. Throughout their affair, Cottingham was raping, killing, and mutilating women and then going home to either his wife or his girlfriend, without a care in the world.

That was the psychopath in him.

"Most serial killers are psychopaths. It is the personality disorder that can allow them to commit a homicide and, then deal with their family as if nothing has happened," said FBI profile Mark Safarik. "One of the attributes that makes them successful in getting away with these crimes is not so much that they're really smart - some are, but many are not - it's that they're psychopaths. They're unaffected emotionally about the crime itself. Twenty minutes after murdering and raping somebody and dumping their body in a ditch, they can act completely normal and be unaffected by the crime. It's this appearance of normalcy that enables them to blend into society. It's not that they're really intelligent. It's just that they make a plan and learn to be better killers from their mistakes."

And if a wife, a girlfriend, and victims weren't enough, Cottingham still had a certain charisma that allowed him to attract other women, who never felt apprehension when approached by the sexual sadist.

"I always had the ability as a young fellow to attract women," he told Fezzani when she visited him at New Jersey State Prison in Trenton, New Jersey.

He attributed his way with the ladies to his fearless approach.

"You know, it's one of those things you can't explain. If I went to a bar, very rarely would I walk out without a woman. Because I could understand the psychiatry, the psychological effect of how to pick up women, what they were looking for. I would always go to the prettiest ones because most men were afraid, and they'd go to the average-looking girl or the average person, the heavyset one that they figure would be an easy catch. I would go for the sharpest girl in the place."

And as his former coworker said, he usually scored. Cottingham was, for whatever reason, a winner.

"Sometimes I'd go out with girls for two, three months, then we'd just part ways," he said casually, not in any way hinting at the words that would follow.

"But sometimes I would kill them. And nobody knew a thing."

A madman hiding in plain sight

That confidence, along with his underlying psychopathy, the characteristic that allowed him come home and eat dinner with his family after committing a murder, made it easy for Cottingham to live a double life.

"Many serial killers hide in plain sight within their communities," according to the FBI. "Serial murderers often have families and homes, are gainfully employed, and appear to be normal members of the community. Because many serial murderers can blend in so effortlessly, they are oftentimes overlooked by law enforcement and the public."

Because they can go quite some time living completely under the radar, it makes them brazen, and that is usually when they slip up.

"As serial killers continue to offend without being captured, they can become empowered, feeling they will never be identified. As the series continues, the killers may begin to take shortcuts when committing their crimes. This often causes the killers to take more chances, leading to identification by law enforcement. It is not that serial killers want to get caught; they feel that they can't get caught," according to the FBI.

It would take Cottingham quite some time to slip up, however.

CHAPTER 4:
Woman's disappearance triggers concern

It was just a few weeks before Christmas of 1977 when Mary Ann Carr went missing from the Ledgeview Terrace apartments where she lived with her husband.

The 26-year-old X-ray technician had been planning to meet with her mother-in-law while her husband was away from home on business, but she never showed up.

By the time her husband returned home family members were frantic, and immediately called the police.

"We received a call that a young married woman was reported missing from her Little Ferry, New Jersey, apartment complex under suspicious circumstances," said Lieutenant Alan Grieco of the Bergen County Sheriff's Department in New Jersey.

When police arrived at the scene, there were no clues as to what might have happened to the pretty X-ray technician.

"There did not appear to be anything broken in the apartment, and we had no indication at all as to what had happened," said Grieco.

There was a witness, a neighbor who lived in the same garden apartments as the Carrs, who saw something strange, however, that for a time put Mary Ann's husband squarely under the police microscope.

"He saw a person in his rear view mirror that he thought was Mary Ann Carr's husband," Grieco said.

Her husband, however, had a solid alibi, and the lead went cold.

It would be years before police realized that Cottingham looked a lot like Mary Ann's husband and connected her murder to him through the calling cards he left behind.

Mary Ann's horrifying last hours

No one knows how Cottingham was able to entice Mary Ann Carr into his vehicle on the day she disappeared. Maybe they talked about the apartment complex, maybe he used Ted Bundy's ruse and pretended to need some help. Whatever the case, Cottingham abducted Mary Ann from the apartment parking lot and then took her to a hotel where he raped, tortured, and murdered her.

He then tossed her body away like so much trash.

On December 16, 1977, Mary Ann Carr's body was found in the parking lot of the Quality Inn Motel, her body dumped between the curb and the chain-link fence surrounding the motel parking lot, Grieco recalled.

"Mary Ann Carr's body had ligature marks on the wrists and the ankles from handcuffs, and she had a ligature mark along her neck," said Philip Calo, who would later serve as the district attorney who prosecuted Richard Cottingham.

Her body was covered in bruises, on her arms, her shoulders, her breasts and thighs, and her right cheek had hemorrhaged, as though she's been struck in the face with a blunt object.

The left leg of her crisp white pants had been cut, and a bunch of her hair, also cut, had fallen onto her right thigh, stark against her light-colored uniform.

According to reports, her shoes, her coat, and her purse were all missing, and residue from tape was found around her mouth.

The most telling evidence, however, was a severe bite mark on her breast, but it would be years before police would be able to recognize that savage bite mark as their killer's gruesome calling card.

Still, the bruises and evidence of sexual assault did not yield enough clues to give officers the solid evidence they needed to track down Mary Ann's killer.

"You have to have the investigation to lead you in a particular direction. Without that direction it's like a shotgun blast," Grieco said.

And it wasn't until later that anyone remembered that Richard Cottingham, who bore more than a striking resemblance to Mary Ann's husband, and his wife, Janet, had lived in the Ledgewood Terrace apartments.

Cottingham flies under the radar, but only for a while

After Mary Ann Carr's murder, police were finding multiple victims of sexual assault near the airport, either along the side of the road or in motel rooms. Some, but not all, of the victims were prostitutes.

All of them, however, had been tortured in a similar way, although police in the neighboring jurisdictions where victims were turning up had not yet connected the dots.

On September 23, 1978, Cottingham again felt the need to satisfy his urges, and barmaid Karen Schilt was his unlucky victim.

The pregnant woman had spent the day working at a bar and grill on Third Avenue called Tuesday's, but she left work at about 6:30 p.m. to visit her boyfriend before returning to work until 8 p.m.

Karen had a few drinks before leaving for another bar on Third Avenue, arriving there at about 8:30 p.m.

It was at this establishment that she struck up a conversation with a guy who called himself John Schaefer, who asked her if she was "a working girl" at some point in their conversation. She said she wasn't, but Schaefer, the pseudonym of choice for Cottingham that night, must have been taken with the girl's looks because it didn't deter him from his mission at all.

Karen tried to ask her drinking companion some questions of her own, but by 9 p.m., just a half hour after sitting down with Cottingham, who attempted to disguise himself by wearing a shaggy wig, she began to feel sick, as though she'd been drugged.

She felt woozy and weak, her stomach was upset, the room had started to spin, and she thought perhaps she was about to faint.

She put down her drink and left the bar, planning on heading home to her apartment. She assumed the man called John Schaefer would stay behind. But he, of course, was already too invested in his victim. His fantasy was already raging in his head, so he got into his car and followed her down Third Avenue.

The chase begins

As he watched her walk, stumbling a bit as she headed for home, he pulled over and asked her if she needed a ride, pretending to be nothing more than a caring new friend.

Karen, too disoriented to make her way home, said yes, and got into Cottingham's car, almost immediately passing out.

When she woke up, they were on the New Jersey turnpike, and Cottingham was shoving three blue and red capsules call Tuinal – the date rape drug of choice before Rohypnol came along - in her mouth and forcing her to swallow them. She then felt a burning pain in her breast before she passed out again.

She was still unconscious at 9 a.m. the next morning, when Little Ferry Police Department Patrolman Raymond Auger found Karen's near-lifeless body stuffed in a drainage ditch behind a car at the Ledgeview Terrace apartment building, the same one where Richard Cottingham had once lived.

Her shirt was pulled up, exposing her breasts, one of which had been burned by a cigarette and brutally bitten, and her pants were undone and pulled down around her ankles.

She was missing her coat, scarf, and purse, and police would later find out a prized ring was also gone.

The 5'5" woman was 22 and pregnant, and her life would never be the same.

Police immediately started CPR, bringing her back from the brink of death, and when Karen finally awoke in a bed at Hackensack Hospital, she could barely remember anything about the night before, thanks to the drugs Cottingham had given her.

Tests concluded she had a cocktail of both secobarbital and amobarbital in her system. Today, secobarbital is one of the most commonly-used drugs in physician-assisted suicide, and was linked to the death of Judy Garland, made famous for her role as Dorothy in "The Wizard of Oz."

With no real clues and little more than a vague description of the man at the bar, police were stymied, and Karen's case would soon grow cold.

Hers would not be the only one.

Another woman survives torturous night with Cottingham

Susan Geiger could have gotten away with never spending "quality" time with Richard Cottingham if she hadn't given him her phone number on October 10, 1978.

But on the night he approached her for a "date," offering her $200 for sex, she was all booked up for the night, so she handed him her digits.

He called the next day, and they set up a time and place to meet.

At midnight in front of the Alpine Motel, Susan met Cottingham. They headed over to the Irish pub Flanagan's on First Street, not far from the Queensboro Bridge.

Once they got settled, Cottingham told Susan his name was Jim, and then offered the truths that he was married with three kids and lived in New Jersey.

He also said he worked in computers, and had won a bunch of money gambling. He showed her his haul, and when she left to visit the restroom, he ordered screwdrivers, thinking the orange juice would mask the taste of the drugs he'd dropped into the drink while she'd been away from the bar.

Almost immediately, things got hazy for Geiger. She remembered riding in a dirty green Thunderbird, she remembered waking up in a hotel room with the man she knew as Jim sexually assaulting her, she recalled being whipped severely with a piece of green garden hose.

She woke up the afternoon of the 12th on the floor of Room 28 of the Airport Motel in Hackensack, New Jersey, bleeding from her vagina, rectum, breasts, face and mouth. Her earrings had been ripped from her ears, and they were also bleeding. Her purse was missing.

Susan called police, and then stumbled out into the sunshine to wait for them to rescue her.

Police again make horrific find

When Captain John Agar of the South Hackensack Police Department pulled up, he saw a woman with her clothing torn and ragged, her lips swollen and bloodied from being savagely beaten, her thoughts incoherent and rambling from having been drugged.

In the room, crime scene analysts found towels stained with semen, which they quickly sent off to the crime lab. The towels revealed a single clue - their suspect was a man with Type O blood.

At Hackensack Hospital, Susan, who was also pregnant, was linked to Karen because her breast had also sustained a serious injury that was clearly a bite.

She was also covered with bruises, likely from the stretch of green garden hose that had been Cottingham's weapon of choice that night.

But bite marks and type O blood were little to go on. Police were again at a dead end.

CHAPTER 5:
Prostitutes made for easy prey

Times Square was a seedy underworld during the years when Richard Cottingham was on the prowl.

And although he sometimes had a specific type that he choose when he went hunting for victim – and many of his first victims were the brunettes with long hair and voluptuous breasts that he loved – he later specifically targeted prostitutes, which were easy to find in nearby New York City, the city that never sleeps.

The city was just recovering from near bankruptcy, and the Rogers and Hammerstein era of "Oklahoma!" had given way to drug dealers, dive bars, hookers, and hourly hotels where they could make a living.

"New York City at that time was a very different place than it is now. The Times Square area was a virtual cesspool," Calo said. "Porno houses up and down the block and streetwalkers for blocks around."

The city's heartbeat was the epitome of urban decay.

Allan Tannenbaum, who worked as a photojournalist for the Soho News around the time that Cottingham was also taking advantage of the girls' desperation, recalled the NYC that was Cottingham's playground.

"It was quite funky, very seedy," he said. Prostitution, "was rampant, it was all over the place. The girls would work on these corners by the subway entrances, close to the peep shows. It was pretty obvious who was a working girl."

But the city was still a draw despite its new dangers, and many of those girls working the streets were from the Midwest and were aspiring to be actors or dancers or singers on Broadway thanks to movies that had glamourized the city as a place where dreams are made.

Midwestern girls were particularly vulnerable

Most of the women working Times Square were Midwestern girls who still harbored hope that they could live the dream life offered by the enticing Big Apple, as intoxicating as Eve's Garden of Eden fruit for those with lives had nothing really going for them. The starry-eyed girls stepped off the bus with super-sized dreams but usually wound up with a pimp instead of a producer.

That's because super-sized dreams come with super-sized budgets, and a lot of those girls arrived with very little money. That made them easy recruits for the pimps who populated the bus stations looking for naïve girls who really had no place to go.

"Many girls would get off the bus nearby and get enticed by pimps who would put them to work," said Tannenbaum, who snapped more than a few documentary-style photographs during his time with the Soho News.

Those girls were often naïve or on drugs, both of which made them easy targets – first for pimps, then for murderers.

They were happy to call Cottingham "master" for a few hours if it meant they were off the streets, and some never imagined that the nondescript guy, slightly pudgy with brown hair cut into a classic '70s style with a deep part, side-swept bangs, and short sideburns was evil incarnate.

Sex workers at high risk for murder

That vulnerability makes sex workers 18 times more likely than other women to be murdered, according to statistics.

"Prostitutes are very common victims. Why? The hardest thing in getting a victim is the abduction," said forensic psychologist Louis Schlesinger. "How do you get a woman to go with you? You have to talk to her, and even if you could talk well and are somewhat articulate and charming and engaging, not all women are going to go with a stranger. The problem with the abduction is eliminated it when targeting a prostitute. Part of their job description is to go with a stranger and take their clothes off and have sex with them."

Gary Ridgway, a truck painter better known as the Green River Killer, chose prostitutes for exactly that reason, because they were easy targets and were unlikely to be immediately missed.

"I picked prostitutes as victims because they were easy to pick up without being noticed," he said. "I knew they would not be reported missing right away and might never be reported missing. I picked prostitutes because I thought I could kill as many of them as I wanted without getting caught."

Their cases are also much more likely to go unsolved, experts say.

According to a 2011 study by Kenna Quinet, a professor at Purdue University Indianapolis's School of Public and Environmental Affairs, called "Prostitutes as Victims of Serial Homicide," not only are prostitutes easy targets for serial killers, almost half of murders where the victim was a prostitute remain unsolved, allowing the killers to continue flying under the radar.

"Prostitute killers amass a greater average number of victims than do non-prostitute killers and when analyzed by decade, those who kill primarily prostitutes, kill for slightly longer periods of time," Quinet wrote in the report.

Cottingham favored prostitutes because they were lured by easy money, and he too believed that they usually had few, if any people who would miss them.

That, of course, is simply not true.

"They're not nobodies," said Lori Townsend, mother of Indiana serial killer Darren Deon Vann's final victim. "They're somebody's daughter, somebody's mother, somebody's sister."

For Cottingham, however, none of that mattered. He didn't care about the families of his victims or the pain he would cause them by taking the life of their loved one. The only thing that was important to him was that he had available to him a victim initially willing to go along with his depraved acts, and that if he hurt them enough, they would struggle in vain to get away. Their desperate contortions, their tears, and their screams silenced by gags, were fast becoming the only thing that aroused him.

CHAPTER 6:
The torture killer

While Richard Cottingham had many depraved qualities – he was a psychopath, a sadist, and a narcissist – he was also a torture killer, a subgroup of sexually sadistic killers who are particularly brutal.

"In reality, killer Richard Cottingham belonged to a subgroup of sexually sadistic serial killers who try to satisfy their self-consuming need for sexual arousal through torturing their victims. The victim's pain and terror are a stimulus to the killer, driving him to a greater frenzy that only serves to intensify the level of the victim's torture until the killer's lust is momentarily satisfied," wrote Robert D. Keppel and William J. Birnes in their book, "Serial Violence: Analysis of Modus Operandi and Signature Characteristics of Killers."

"To get to this level of sexual gratification, torture killers are most adept at luring victims, capturing them and then springing their traps. Most are smooth talkers and beguilingly charming but deceitful and ultimately lethal. Torture killers use all sorts of conventional and innovative approaches to con their victims into a false feeling of safety. They flatter and flirt, offer rewards – especially money – hold out the promise of satisfying exactly what they perceive the victim wants, and speak directly to the victim's needs. It's all a ruse made to look innocent to trick a potential victim into stepping into the killer's world."

Since Cottingham targeted prostitutes, he was able to lure them first with money, wads of cash he said he'd won playing poker, then by offering false sympathy – he was incapable of feeling sympathetic about his victims' pain – and then by telling stories about himself that made him seem safe and nonthreatening.

The games sadists play

According to Dr. Elizabeth Yardley, Director of the Centre for Applied Criminology at Birmingham City University in England, that ruse – appearing friendly, perhaps vulnerable – is all part of the twisted game torture killers play.

"Apparent vulnerability and the need to please have been used effectively time and time again by serial killers as a way of hiding a sinister personality," she said. "Some of the world's best known serial killers have a frightening ability to manipulate those around them, pressing the right buttons in order to present themselves in a false light."

Of course, with prostitutes, the offer of money – especially generous amounts of money for what they perceived to be a little bondage and sex with a guy who liked to be called "master" – was an easy way to lure victims, even seasoned prostitutes who have learned a thing or two about who to trust and who represents danger out on the streets.

It is then that the killer begins what Keppel and Birnes call "the three D's: dependency, or forcing the victim to rely upon the killer in order to survive; dread, which is an obvious result of the terror a victim must feel over the pain and torture their captor is reveling in; degradation, which is common for torture killers who want to humiliate their victims as they force them to do whatever deranged thing fills his fantasy life; and drugs, which are commonly used to keep victims from having the strength or wherewithal to escape.

Cottingham was seen as the ultimate torture killer.

"His crimes – violent attacks and murders – are some of the cruelest I've ever come across," said Nadia Fezzani.

Empathy? Surprisingly yes, say two experts

While it would seem unimaginable that a torture killer – a person who revels in the agony of others – could possess empathy, that particular quality is what makes their crimes so devious and dark.

According to Jack Levin and James Alan Fox in the book "Serial Murder and the Psychology of Violent Crimes," sadistic serial killers have to have empathy for their victims, even a heightened sense of empathy, because understanding their pain is what gives them so much pleasure and allows them to more easily coerce their victims.

"We believe that lack of empathy is one characteristic of sadistic killers that has been accepted far too uncritically by psychologists and criminologists alike," the two wrote. "Many investigators have indeed argued, based on superficial familiarity with serial murder cases, that sadistic serial killers are incapable of appreciating their victims' pain and suffering."

Cottingham himself said killing was little more than a game, but it was a high stakes game that was solely focused on his pleasure.

"Killers who do not understand their victims' feelings would be incapable of conning them effectively. For example, Theodore Bundy understood all too well the sensibilities of female college students who were taken in by his feigned helplessness," Levin and Fox wrote. "He trapped attractive young women by appearing to be disabled and asking them for help.

"Second, a well-honed sense of emotional empathy is critical for a sadistic killer's enjoyment of the suffering of his victims. For sadistic objectives to be realized, a killer who tortures, sodomizes, rapes, and humiliates must be able to both understand and experience his victim's suffering. Otherwise, there would be no enjoyment or sexual arousal. Thus, he feels his victim's pain, but he interprets it as his own pleasure. Indeed, the more empathic he is, the greater his enjoyment of his victim's suffering."

Don't get it twisted. Empathy and sympathy are not the same

But empathy, the understanding of the pain he was causing his victims, is not to be confused with sympathy.

Cottingham understood that his victims felt pain, but that was his pleasure. He certainly didn't feel bad about it.

"Cottingham is pretty much a very classic serial sexual murderer," said Schlesinger. "The best way to understand serial sexual murderer, sex and aggression become fused and the aggressive act becomes eroticized.

"In regular sexual intercourse there is some level of pain," Schlesinger added. For serial sexual murders, the erotic pain of a gentle bite, nails scratching across a back, for example, become the nipples Cottingham nearly severed from most of his victims as he watched their faces contort in pain, tears rain from their eyes. All of it gave him the arousal he needed to then continue the torture with brutal rapes.

"These really take on a life of their own," Schlesinger said of the paraphilia and erotic triggers that excite serial sexual murderers.

"Years after Cottingham had been put away," said Keppel, who studied numerous serial killers including Ted Bundy and Gary Ridgeway, "as I tried to figure out what could drive the sexually sadistic serial killer subtype, I kept asking myself what it was that ultimately intrigued me about the Cottingham cases. Partly it was the level of sadistic torture that Cottingham acted out on his victims. He didn't kill them and desecrate their bodies, he forced them to experience pain and humiliation before he killed them. Then he desecrated their bodies."

Death wasn't Cottingham's true motivation, torture was, which is why some of his victims survived to take the stand after Cottingham was captured and put on trial.

If the victim died before Cottingham was fully satisfied, he then turned his attentions to the corpse, defiling his victims' bodies in unimaginably horrific ways.

"I never had encountered this kind of dark evil in any of the subjects I covered. I had written about some deeply disturbed people, but not anyone who was as treacherous and deviant as Cottingham," said Rod Leith, who covered the Cottingham case from start to finish for the Bergen County Record and later penned two books about his experiences.

CHAPTER 7:
A murder that became unforgettable

If torture murders weren't terrible enough, just over a year later, Richard Cottingham took his depravity to an almost unimaginable new level.

Toward the end of November in 1979, a man registered as Carl Wilson of Merlin, New Jersey, had booked a room at the Travel Inn Motor Lodge, now the Travel Inn Hotel New York on 42nd Street, just two blocks from Times Square, making it a perfect spot for a guy looking to spend some private time indulging in some dark fantasies.

The man, in his 30s, was tall with sandy hair, and staff remembered that he placed the "Do Not Disturb" sign on the door of Room 417 and was not seen again.

In fact, the room was quiet for four days, and hotel guests and staffers had no idea the depravity happening behind that closed door.

After booking the room, Cottingham picked up two prostitutes, 23-year-old Deedeh Goodarzi, an immigrant from Kuwait with dark hair and high cheekbones who was working as a prostitute to make money to support herself and her infant child, and another woman in her teens or early 20s who remains a Jane Doe, and took them to his room.

It was December 2, 1979, a cold day in New York City, and the two women were likely happy to get off the street for a while and get warm, even if it meant paying for their comfort by satisfying Cottingham's carnal pleasures.

Goodarzi, blessed with thick, dark hair with soft waves, was the mother of a four-month-old baby, and times were likely tough for the immigrant mom.

But she and her fellow working girl likely had no idea the horrors they would experience in that hotel room before they died.

Torture becomes a sick game

Both women had been raped and tortured. Strange slash marks covered their torsos, but the wounds were shallow, done to cause pain and illicit fear but not to kill.

"The thing that's important, there were no penetrating wounds," said forensic pathologist Dr. Louis Napolitano, who described seeing curved cuts around the women's breasts, straight cuts beneath them.

"There were no knife wounds that penetrated into the body. There were all superficial. He's teasing them. 'I'm not doing anything to you to kill you right away. I'm not putting a knife in your chest or cutting or making you die right away. No, I want you to know I'm here doing things to you,'" Napolitano said. "He's doing things to them to make them afraid, to have them subjugate to him. 'I'm doing this to you and I can make it worse.'"

After Cottingham had had his fun torturing his victims, binding them together, inciting unimaginable fear, he savagely raped and murdered them.

Cottingham then mutilated their bodies by removed their hands and heads, and placed the women separately on the room's twin beds before he sprinkled an accelerant on the torsos and set fire to the hotel room.

"The bodies had been desecrated," said Grieco.

There was some attention paid to detail, however, because the women's clothes were folded neatly in the tub, the same level of attention he'd paid to the clothing of Nancy Vogel, although police did not make the connection at the time.

"Nobody knew who was responsible," added Colo. "It was a mystery."

For Nadia Fezzani, who booked the room prior to her interview with Richard Cottingham in prison to get a sense of how those last hours might have been for the women, the space immediately caused her to feel the hairs on the back of her neck rise as a shiver ran down her spine. She intuitively knew she was standing in a place of pure evil, sorrow and unimaginable horror.

"This is where it happened. I don't like it here," she said in an episode of the French program "Investigations and Revelations," which included much of her interview with Cottingham. "Not a good feeling. I feel like I'm in a horror film."

She was not far from wrong. Cottingham's crimes seemed snatched from the screens of some of the goriest and grotesque of horror movies, and he reveled in attempting to make his scenes the most macabre the world had ever seen.

All fun and games

For Cottingham, however, the entire business was entertainment, a night of joviality in which he alone had the fun.

"I enjoyed it. It was a game," he told Fezzani. "It's scary to a girl, to have something done like that, to be so close to a knife, so to speak, pressed against you. The situations that I was seeking were more of a power trip. What I was doing was something like a power trip. The power of holding someone's fate in your hands is a very powerful aphrodisiac. The adrenalin rush is …. You're in complete control of somebody's destiny."

For the two prostitutes who'd hoped to get out of the cold and escape what was then a seedy Times Square, their destiny was death, and for the Jane Doe, it would be a death that would never be acknowledged.

Deedeh Goodarzi, who had gone by the street names Jacqueline Thomas, Jackie Thomas, Sabrina Roberts and Crystal Roberts, would be identified through X-rays.

The only thing anyone would know about the second victim was that she was young, she weighed approximately 110 pounds, and on the last day of her life, she had chosen a pair of Bonjour jeans, a mohair sweater in a shade of dark burgundy, and black patent leather boots as her outfit of choice, topped by a black, full-length coat.

Police hung posters with photographs of Jane Doe's clothing in hopes that someone would recognize them and help them identify the girl, but no one came forward with any information.

Hiding evidence in plain sight

While the slow cuts he made with his knife were his version of sensual foreplay leading up to a vicious rape, Cottingham cut off the victim's heads and hands for more matter-of-fact reasons, so his victims would be harder to identify.

"That was done only to prevent identification," he said.

These, he carried away in a duffel bag, as casually as if it was gym clothes or bowling shoes.

"I had nerves of steel," he told Fezzani, his voice proud as he remembered the incident, no trace of guilt or regret in his voice. "When I disposed of the heads, I took them out of the hotel. Two cops pull me over, they see me with a carryall bag at 3:30 in the morning, they asked me what I was doing. I said I was staying in the hotel and was going to get something to eat. Without batting an eye, they would believe me. They never asked what was in the bag or for any ID or anything like that. I could make people believe what they wanted to believe. It's godlike almost."

Yes, it's safe to say that Cottingham was the epitome of a narcissist.

Firefighters arrive to find unspeakable horror

By the time firefighter James Rogers had reached the fourth floor of the Travel Motor Lodge, the smoke was a thick, dark, impenetrable wall.

He saw two bodies, one on each of the room's twin beds, and he grabbed the one closest to the door first.

"I carried her out the door and put her down on the hall floor," Rogers told the New York Daily News. "I was preparing to give mouth-to-mouth resuscitation, which is standard procedure, when I suddenly noticed there was no head."

The second victim had fared no better, and she, too, was without a head.

"I'm used to seeing charred bodies," Rogers said, "but this was the worst experience I've ever had in 12 years of firefighting. I've never come across something like that. I hope I never do again."

Rogers was a 15-year veteran of the New York City Fire Department when he entered that hotel room fire. He later underwent trauma counseling because of the horror of what he had seen.

The blaze had started because someone had soaked what remained of the women's bodies with lighter fluid and set them on fire.

The head and hands had been removed with the precision of a surgeon, suggesting that the killer hadn't rushed the job, but instead had savored every sick minute of it.

Again, a detective told a reporter with the New York Times that the crime scene, despite the desecration, had been swept clean of clues and in terms of evidence, was one of the most effectively swept rooms he'd ever seen.

The Times Square Ripper revealed?

At the insurance company where Cottingham worked, everyone was talking about the gruesome murders.

"This guy, his name is Rob, came in and said, 'What sick son of a bitch would do something like this, take the heads and hands of a girl and set the beds on fire?' I looked at Richard, and he said, 'I don't know Rob, it could have been you, it could have been me.' I thought it was a joke," said Dominick Volpe, shuddering slightly as he remembered that day in 1979.

Meanwhile, police in New Jersey were not making any connection to Cottingham and the murder of Mary Ann Carr, because the cases were so very different.

"It did not seem to have any connection to our case," said Grieco. "With the bodies being desecrated as they were, there was no connection at the time."

The murder of Mary Ann was less savage, so Grieco had no real reason to think that the horrific crime scene so close to NYC's Times Square was connected to his case.

Escalating depravity a common trait

But sexual serial killers usually have one terrible thing in common. What is arousing at the beginning – rape and murder, for example – becomes less so, and the murders that follow tend to be more savage and complex.

That progression is normal for the majority of sexual serial killers, according to Louis Schlesinger.

They are like drug addicts in that they need more and more to feed their habit.

And sometimes their drug of choice, so to speak, changes.

"About 70 percent of serial sexual murders will experiment at a crime scene and do something very, very different with one victim that they had not done with the others such as cut their eyes out or cut their vaginas out and so on," he said. "When an investigator without extensive experience in this field looks at it, one victim looks so very different that they're lead to believe, at least from their own experience, that it has to be someone else. That's incorrect."

And that simple, understandable mistake is one of the myriad things that allow many serial killers to operate under police radar for years, leaving a trail of dead bodies behind them in their wake.

CHAPTER 8:
A return to hotel hell

On May 5, 1980, Maryann Sancanelli, a housekeeper at the Quality Inn Motel in Hasbrough Heights, New Jersey, was cleaning Room 132 when she noticed that although one of the room's two beds had not been slept in, the bedspread was crooked and pulled down at the foot.

When she tried to vacuum beneath the bed, her vacuum hit something rather large, an object that was big enough to block the foot of the bed.

It was then that she noticed a stench in the room that luckily for her, was unfamiliar.

"She detected what she was a foul odor coming from the bed area. Lifting the mattress from the frame, she was startled to see the naked, handcuffed body of a naked, deceased female lying there," said Grieco.

The woman, who would turn out to be 19-year-old Valerie Ann Street, was a pretty girl with a slender waist and large, perky breasts that were jutting out as if she'd been arranged that way, her cuffed hands twisted beneath her. She was 5'4", about 135 pounds, with faux strawberry blond hair that hung down to her shoulders. And she had clearly been through hell before she died.

Street had been tortured severely, and the handcuffs that held her hands behind her back were so tight that they had left deep marks around her wrists – raw, red gouges that resembled gory bracelets. Her body was covered in an array of marks including bruises, slashes, stabbing cuts and bite marks that had nearly severed her left nipple.

Her agony had likely lasted for hours, based on the marks left behind on her ravaged body.

She'd likely wanted to scream, but if she had, her cries were muffled, because police later found the residue of tape surrounding her mouth, which was slightly open, partially covered by her dyed hair.

Her neck had two ligature marks, suggesting that after her killer had finished torturing and raping her, he'd killed her by strangulation, intimately watching her as her eyes went slowly from desperation to death.

"On her lower back, there was an abrasion which had been made by a sharp object that we thought at the time was a knife," said Calo.

"Those were torture marks," said Schlesinger. "It's eroticized, the power and control that the offender has over the victim, to make the victim realize that he, the offender, is in control of life and death. So oftentimes the offender will prolong her agony, to kill her in a very slow and deliberate way so that she's aware that he's going to kill her."

All her clothing and any identification that she might have been carrying with her were missing.

"It was extremely frightening and disturbing to the chambermaid, to say the least," said Grieco.

Evidence begins to add up

When Dr. Louis Napolitano of the Bergen County Medical Examiner's Office conducted his autopsy, he found that Valerie had suffered a severe blow to the right side of her head that had caused head trauma and had been tortured over a 24-hour period before her death, based on her wounds.

For more than a month, Valerie was held in the Bergen County morgue, because the only evidence left behind in the room was a single latent fingerprint on the set of handcuffs and a broken piece of earring.

The hotel registry provided no clues, and no one knew her identity.

Although Valerie had registered for the room herself, she'd used the pseudonym Shelley Dudley. She'd checked in at about 4:30 p.m. on May 4, and never checked out.

She was eventually identified by her fingerprints, which turned up in Florida crime files for a conviction on prostitution charges.

Valerie had only been in New York City for four days. She'd left Florida on April 30, and on May 3 was working the corner of Madison Avenue and 32nd Street. A prostitute named China said she'd last seen Valerie on May 4, on the same corner.

But in her death, Valerie offered a very big clue that would help speed police as they attempted to catch a killer.

"That was the second case of a woman's body being found on the premises of this particular hotel," said Grieco, who had not forgotten that Mary Ann Carr's body had been found in the parking lot of the same motel.

This would be evidence that he would add to his burgeoning pile of information, and his cold case grew is little bit warmer.

It proved that the killer, if the cases did indeed align, was so brazen in his belief that he would not be caught that he took careless chances to test police.

"I think that he used the same hotel is narcissism," said Dr. Katherine Ramsland, who said that Cottingham was so delusional in his narcissistic thinking that he truly felt that he was above the law.

"They're so superior to everybody else that there's no chance they're going to get caught," Ramsland said. "Some narcissists absolutely believe they are invisible, untouchable."

Time between crimes escalates

As with most serial killers, the act of taking a life is seductive and addictive, and they crave more and more experiences, usually as a way to bring a long-held fantasy to life.

"With serial killers, there's usually a cooling off period, and that cooling off period tends to get shorter and shorter as time goes on," according to Dr. Michael Aamodt, head of the psychology department at Virginia's Radford University and an expert on serial killers.

Cottingham's cooling off period had decreased significantly, and just over a week later, on May 12, 1980, Cottingham dumped cocktail waitress Pamela Weisenfeld in a parking lot in Teaneck, New Jersey.

She had been drugged and beaten, and her breasts were also savagely bitten.

A gruesome second fire

It was only 10 days after Valerie Ann Street, May 15, 1980, that firefighters were again called to a hotel – this time the Seville on East 29th Street – where they again found a mutilated young woman with multiple, deep bite marks marring her body.

She had also been set on fire as a way to erase certain evidence.

And although the killer had left her head and her hands, her breasts had both been neatly sliced off and arranged on the headboard.

He had, like many killers, taken things a step further into depravity, in part to gain notoriety and attention, but also to satisfy urges that were becoming increasingly hard to satisfy.

"In almost all serial sexual murder cases they will go above and beyond killing the person and engage in postmortem activity that to them is sexually gratifying. This type of ritualistic behavior grows out of the suspect's fantasy life," said Schlesinger.

It grows more elaborate as the killer becomes more comfortable killing, especially as he brings his fantasies out of his head and acts them out on his unwilling victims.

"Very often as a series of murders occur, the individual's behavior becomes much more elaborate as the offender becomes much more comfortable with killing. The ritualistic behavior is apt to become more personalized and embellished," Schlesinger said.

They are working to get it right, experts say.

"Serial killers keep on killing because they develop and embellish this fantasy until they have the perfect murder," added Dr. Ron Holmes, an Oregon-based coroner.

Fingerprints, photos lead to victim's identification

Based on fingerprints, and after being identified through photos, the victim was later identified as 25-year-old Jean Reyner, a prostitute who worked the derelict Times Square area.

So strong were the similarities between Reyner's murder and the earlier case that police had no doubt that it was the handiwork of the same killer.

The calling card was clear due to the bites and the fire that charred Jean's flesh.

But the killer had also spent some time cleaning up after his crime, and had virtually sterilized the room in an effort to keep from leaving behind any identifying clues like some careless criminals.

One detective repeated the earlier words about Cottingham's other crime scene that included fire, and said he had never seen a room so thoroughly cleaned.

Although police were sure the murder was the work of a man now dubbed the "Times Square Ripper" or "The Torso Killer," depending on what news outlet was reporting on it, they had a sense of despair over how they were ever going to track their slippery, faceless suspect.

What they had – two hotels, at least four savagely mutilated women, three of them burned, and a suspect that might just as well be invisible.

But finally there was a solid link between Valerie Ann Sheet, the women burned in the NYC hotel room and the unsolved Carr case from back in 1977.

And police in both jurisdictions would not be puzzled for very long.

Trouble in 'paradise'

As police began piecing together an artful, evil, and complex puzzle, at the Cottingham home, there were signs of trouble.

Perhaps the girlfriend of two years had gotten to Janet, because in April of 1980, Cottingham's wife had filed for divorce, charging him with "extreme cruelty," especially for his refusal to have sex with her since late 1976.

By then, it was likely that he was only able to get off while in the throes of savage sex, and he couldn't let Janet in on his secrets.

His wife alleged he at times left the family without money for essentials and would not come home until 4 a.m. or 5 a.m., even though his shift at Blue Cross Blue Shield ended at 11 p.m., and he had chosen to go on vacation alone, leaving his family at home to swelter in the New Jersey heat. The complaint also alleged he visited Plato's Retreat, a heterosexual swingers club in Manhattan, and was a habitual patron of the gay bars and the bathhouses that peppered Manhattan.

Cottingham wasn't happy at all about the unrest at home, and somebody would have to pay.

CHAPTER 9:
Leslie Ann O'Dell suffers to save countless victims

Leslie Ann O'Dell, a blond who stood just 5'4", had only been working the corner of Lexington Avenue and 25th Street for about a week when she encountered Richard Cottingham.

Just a few blocks from where Marilyn Monroe filmed her iconic subway grate scene in "The Seven Year Itch," O'Dell had arrived in the Big Apple by bus, having left her home state of Washington four days earlier, making the cross-country journey in hopes of living a better life.

Unfortunately, she became one of the naïve girls picked up by pimps at the bus station and was immediately put to work in one of the seedier sections of town.

Like all the others, she'd arrived in town with very little money, just some long-held hopes for something different than what she'd known on the West Coast.

The pimps knew their targets, and Leslie was easy prey. Unfortunately, the pretty 18-year-old also fit the description of what Cottingham liked in a girl.

He called himself Tommy.

And when he offered to take her out first, the girl had no idea that she would soon be fighting very hard for her life, no matter how she'd felt about it a few weeks earlier, when she'd ditched everything she ever knew and took a risk on the Big Apple.

Cottingham first plied her with drinks as he droned on about his computer job and the house in the suburbs he had up until a month ago shared with his family, talking until nearly 3 a.m.

He then played upon her desperation and offered to help her escape her situation in New York City by taking her to a bus terminal in New Jersey, away from the dangerous and powerful pimps who already controlled her.

Hope, rising

The grateful girl accepting Cottingham's offer, and was likely formulating a new plan for her life as they drove over the George Washington Bridge into Jersey.

They stopped at an all-night diner called New Star Diner where Cottingham bought Leslie a steak, and they talked some more, until eventually Leslie agreed to have sex with the man she now saw as her rescuer for $100, money that would help her get away from her dangerous situation.

She didn't even think that what was to come would be worse than anything she had experienced in the past week.

The sun was coming up when Cottingham left Leslie in the car and checked into the Hasbrouck Heights Quality Inn Motor Hotel, the same place he had left his last victim, Valerie Ann Street, stuffed beneath the mattress less than three weeks early.

Unfortunately for Leslie, the clerk didn't recognize Cottingham as he handed over the keys to room 117.

Keys in hand, Cottingham drove to the back of the motel and the two entered through a back door. He left Leslie in the room, telling her he wanted to move his vehicle to a more secure location, and he returned with a bottle of whiskey and a bag.

Cottingham offered to give the Leslie a massage before they got started, and the exhausted girl rolled onto her stomach.

"He said he wanted to be my friend," she said. But friendship was the last thing Cottingham intended to offer the girl.

He straddled her back as if to begin massaging her, but instead pulled a knife from his bag and held it to her throat to subdue her while he handcuffed her wrists together behind her back.

He straddled her and began his torture routine, telling her that he derived pleasure out of torturing women, and that she was a whore and deserved every bit of the pain he was about to inflict upon her.

He flipping her over, made his first cut with his knife, and told her that he would soon be burning her breasts, her genitals, and her anus, taking delight in her pain and her struggles to escape.

This was the part Cottingham liked best, eliciting screams and terror from his victims, exacting a rage-filled form of punishment that he reserved for certain types of women.

He especially loved punishing prostitutes.

"Prostitutes are sexual service providers, and that offends many serial sexual murderers," said Schlesinger. "As ironic as it sounds, many serial sexual murders view themselves as highly moralistic and want to degrade prostitutes for behaving in what they consider to be impermissible sexual conduct," said Schlesinger. "They're very mixed up sexually, so you would think they would understand prostitutes and relate to them, but they don't. They have a very twisted sense of sexuality."

During torture, Cottingham said he enjoyed it, making superficial teasing stab marks on the bodies of his victims.

"It's a power trip, an adrenalin rush and aphrodisiac. You're in complete control of someone's destiny," Cottingham told Nadia Fezzani.

As Leslie struggled to understand what was happening to her, she felt Cottingham's teeth on her nipple, drawing blood, as he sank himself into her, beginning what would be hours of torture.

He bit her savagely, nearly tearing her nipple off as he pulled, and then licked her blood.

Over the next several hours, Cottingham raped and sodomized Leslie, forced her to give him oral sex, beat her, sliced her with his knife, and escalated her levels of terror.

All the while he talked about the many ways she would suffer, much like the Toy Box Killer David Parker Ray did with his victims, who woke from unconsciousness, often strapped into a chair with their legs spread wide, to hear Ray's voice on a tape recording, going into vivid detail about the rules he required his new slaves to live by unless they wanted to be whipped or tortured in other barbaric ways.

The talking turned Cottingham on, and played a role in his torture.

"He told me to shut up, that I was a whore and I had to be punished," Nancy later recounted as she sat on the witness stand. "He said the other girls took it, and I had to take it, too. He said that uncountable times."

Between bouts of torture, the rape, the sodomy, and forcing his penis down her throat violently, between the biting, the beatings, slashing her with his knife and whipping with a leather belt, Cottingham would take time to wipe Leslie's face with a damp washcloth, either to sooth her or to bring her back from delirium so he could again take pleasure in her agony.

At one point when her hands weren't handcuffed, Nancy reached under the bed to grab the gun Cottingham had threatened her with, and attempted to shoot the man who had been terrorizing her for hours.

The gun was fake and didn't fire. It did give Cottingham an edge, however, and he grabbed the knife that he had put down in order to have his fill of Nancy sexually.

Nancy's screams filled the room.

"I screamed, 'Oh, God, no!' I just screamed for my life," she said.

Leslie had endured hours of unmentionable torture before her cries alerted another guest in the hotel. That person called the front desk and reported hearing screams coming from Room 117 at around 9:30 a.m.

Luck for Cottingham finally runs out

The front desk clerk responded quickly and called police, and then raced to the room and demanded that Cottingham, who had registered with a fake name, open the door.

"It took several minutes for someone to be coaxed to the door," Grieco said.

When the door did open, only slightly, it revealed a terrified Leslie, who had been instructed by Cottingham to say that she was fine before he positioned himself behind her.

"Richard Cottingham was standing behind her where he couldn't be seen, but he had a knife into her side," Grieco said.

When asked if she was okay, Leslie said yes, but her eyes told a different story.

"With her eyes, she gave the impression that everything was not okay," Grieco said. "She moved them right to left, indicated that there was a problem."

"She couldn't say anything because he was right there with her, but she managed to get a message out, and she outsmarted him," reporter Rod Leith added.

Cottingham had gotten careless

This time, Cottingham had allowed the pleasure he received from hearing his victim scream override his desire not to get caught.

He was so aroused by Leslie's cries of pain, anguish, and fear that he failed to register how loud they were, and that had made him careless.

"When they remain at large for weeks, months, even years, they can indeed feel superior to the police, so much so that they cut corners a little bit," according to James Alan Fox, a criminologist at Northeastern University in Boston.

It was surprising, though, given the detail that Cottingham included in his crime scenes, like painting a deranged portrait in blood and dismemberment that required just one last sick element to make it memorable.

"When a serial killer is disappointed by a failure to experience his ultimate fantasy in real life exactly the way he envisioned it in his mind, he will continue to kill in an attempt to achieve the ideal fantasy. Such is the obsessive, compulsive and cyclical nature of serial murder," said Bonn.

Leslie's was likely going to be his piece de resistance, if only she'd kept quiet. But by making so much noise, she not only saved her own life, but also the lives of many of the other prostitutes working Times Square in the late 1970s and early 1980s.

"The number one way serial killers are apprehended is by a surviving victim, especially early on in a killing series, when the offender has not yet perfected his technique," said Schlesinger.

The great escape foiled

Although Cottingham attempted to flee, and ran out the back door, his bag of torture devices clutched in his hand, he was apprehended by police before he got very far.

"At the time of his arrest, he had handcuffs, tape — it was either to place over their mouths or to bind their hands or feet or whatever," said Dean Conway, who would become

Cottingham's defense attorney for his first of four trials in two states.

The bag also contained a leather gag, two slave collars, a switchblade, replica pistols, and a stockpile of prescription pills including Valium and barbiturates.

Based on much of the evidence, including the motel where Leslie was found – the same hotel where Mary Ann Carr's body was found – arresting officers alerted Grieco, who felt waves of relief when the call came in.

"There was great deal of excitement when we got the call that a suspect had been apprehended attempting to leave the motel," Grieco said.

Alan Grieco and Ed Denning had the pleasure of arresting Cottingham, a man they'd been haunted by ever since they'd found Mary Ann Carr's lifeless body tossed carelessly against the Jersey parking lot's chain link fence.

CHAPTER 10:
The interrogation

Cottingham was read his rights and then told officers that the sex with Leslie Ann was consensual, and that she had agreed to let him do anything he wanted for $180.

Certainly nearly biting off her nipple – a calling card that Cottingham seemingly required in order to achieve sexual satisfaction – was reasonable, given the free reign his $180 payment had given him over Leslie Ann's defenseless body.

Grieco and Denning, experienced in the art of interrogation, tried to read their suspect.

When it comes to dealing with psychopaths, however, the rules are very different.

"Psychopaths are not sensitive to altruistic interview themes, such as sympathy for their victims or remorse/guilt over their crimes. They do possess certain personality traits that can be exploited, particularly their inherent narcissism, selfishness, and vanity. Specific themes in past successful interviews of psychopathic serial killers focused on praising their intelligence, cleverness, and skill in evading capture," according to the FBI.

Essentially, telling offenders how smart they were for evading capture for so long sometimes feeds their egos enough that they spill their entire story.

Denning and Grieco tried to play on that by showing sympathy for Cottingham, who as a narcissist believed that nothing at all was his fault.

"He was sitting there with Alan and I, and I was holding his hand and trying to get him to confess," Denning said. "His eyes welled up and he said, 'I have a problem with women.'"

He said little more.

Attempted murder called consensual

He told officers that the encounter with Leslie was so savage because he was stressed about his divorce hearing, which he'd gone to the courthouse to attend, only to have it postponed.

He said he then went to see a movie – he didn't remember what theater – and also went to a restaurant to grab a bite to eat.

What restaurant, investigators asked? Cottingham also didn't remember that.

Afterwards, he told cops he went to a bar on Times Square, the Blarney Stone, and grabbed a drink. He then went to another bar for another drink.

He told them that Leslie Ann had approached him there, and they'd agreed on the sum of $180, and after a few other stops, they went to the hotel, where he registered under the name Caruthers.

He then began referring to Leslie Ann as "the female subject," something many serial killers do, because they don't see their victims as humans, but instead as essentially toys.

"When questioned about details as to the location and places that he frequents, and so on, he was evasive and consistently said I cannot recall or I don't remember," said Denning.

It was all a game, he said.

"At no time during this period did she object to any of these sexual acts," Cottingham told police. "I just started playing the game."

The handcuffs, he said, were for his own sexual pleasure.

The ankle cuffs, "were to keep her from running away if she got panicky," he told detectives.

As for the knife, "I pointed the knife towards her and told her not to make any noise."

But threatening? Of course not.

"The handcuffs and other paraphernalia were just something I kept on hand," he said, matter of fact, as if the items were absolutely normal.

"It was just one of the games I like to play, and I wanted to see how it feels to have someone under control," he said.

Police knew it was no game for Leslie, however, especially given the damage she'd suffered during her hours of torture.

"He sodomized her, he beat her very, very severely, he bit her breasts, very severely," said Bergen County District Attorney Dennis Calo.

The evidence was incriminating, and Cottingham had no explanation for it.

So instead of talking, he lawyered up.

When defense attorney Dean Conway first got a good look at his client, he was not impressed by what he saw.

"He was at least average looking, but like I said, kind of stocky. Well built, you might say," Conway said.

And Conway didn't appreciate Cottingham's unwillingness to take responsibility for his actions, giving the giant pile of evidence facing him, from Leslie Ann's ravaged body to the bag of sadistic toys he'd carried with him as he tried to flee.

"He just flat out denied it," said Conway. "I found it very difficult to accept. They sort of caught him red handed, one might say."

Questioning goes cold

Police, finally comparing notes between jurisdictions, questioned him about the places he'd lived and the murders he was now suspected of committing based on his modus operandi.

Cottingham, however, was tough.

"I know you are doing your job, but I know what you're trying to do," he said. "You are trying to trick me and you're being nice to me because you want me to admit to things I didn't do. Aren't you guys going to beat me like they do in New York?"

He then let officials know exactly how he planned to spend the rest of the interrogation.

"I don't have to say anything," he told officers.

A treasure trove of trophies

While their subject wouldn't talk, his home would have plenty to say.

And it, the lower portion of a two-family home including a locked basement room, was much more forthcoming than the killer.

Grieco and Denning obtained a warrant and quickly uncovered Cottingham's secrets.

"We wound up searching the premises and he had a private room down here," said Grieco. "The only one who had access to it was Cottingham. He wouldn't let his wife or his children in here."

But in Cottingham's basement, the things they found horrified the seasoned officers.

"He seemed to be a normal dad and husband," said Grieco. "It's what we didn't know was hidden underneath. He truly was a monster."

To everyone involved, it was a true Jekyll and Hyde case.

"Cottingham had two personalities. He went into his job as a computer tech, minded his own business, went home, then he'd go out in the evening and canvas Manhattan scenes, looking for victims," said Rod Leith.

Souvenirs of death

The items included a tiny koala bear that Valerie Ann Street carried with her, perhaps as a reminder of happier, more innocent years, the earrings of which they'd previously recovered a broken bit and an apartment key that fit the door of Mary Ann Carr's apartment.

"He had in this room, souvenirs or memorabilia, or whatever you want to call it," Conway said. "Items that he took from these women after he tortured them and murdered them."

Trophies are common for serial killers, and Cottingham was hardly the first serial killer to have a hiding place for his mementos of death.

Many serial killers have a locked place where they hide evidence of their crimes. Jerry Brudos kept his treasures, including photographs and a frozen foot, in a locked garage, and his wife was only allowed to communicate through an intercom system when he was in there, and only he had the keys. John Wayne Gacy had a basement crawlspace, and his wife was forbidden to venture down there. He told her the area was full of rodents, which was an easy ploy to keep her away. Jeffrey Dahmer took photos of his victims, often in the middle of dismemberment, which he kept in a drawer of his nightstand, close enough to use for masturbation sessions.

"People that we refer to as organized killers will often take trophies from their victims, an earring or a shoe," said Schlesinger. "Like big game hunters, the trophy room helps them remember those moments when they felt most in control. It's the place where they can go to indulge in their most sadistic fantasies of what they'd done to other people."

For Rod Leith, that trophy room was one of the most horrifically graphic elements of the case.

"I got to know law enforcement in county and municipalities, breaking news about this guy. The most fascinating thing at first was that he was taking items from his victims, and putting them in his rented Lodi home. He was putting jewelry ... earrings, rings ... in his room as tokens of his 'accomplishments.'"

Leith was not the only one involved in the case who was disturbed by the finds.

"Some people might have trophies for their exploits in baseball or basketball or golf. These were his trophies, these were his criminal activities which he had gotten away with, and these were his trophies about how intelligent he was, how charming he was, and how much smarter he was than everybody else," said Calo grimly.

Charges pile up quickly

While Cottingham was initially charged only with holding Leslie against her will, his charges grew as officers learned more about the heinous man they were holding in their custody.

Within days, based on the items found in Cottingham's basement chamber of horrors and in his car, Bergen County law enforcement officials were trading notes with New York City police, who were still a bit shell-shocked by the two prostitutes who had been beheaded and burned in a Times Square Hotel, and were looking for answers.

New York cops soon determined that Cottingham was not only responsible for those murders, but also was the lead suspect in the May 5 mutilation murder of Valerie Ann Street and the May 15, 1980, murder of Jean Reyner, whose breasts had been removed before her body was lit on fire.

Based on the growing pile of evidence shared between New Jersey and New York police, Cottingham was charged with kidnapping, attempted murder, aggravated assault, aggravated assault with a deadly weapon, aggravated sexual assault while armed (rape), aggravated sexual assault while armed (sodomy), aggravated sexual assault while armed (fellatio), possession of a weapon, possession of controlled dangerous substances, Secobarbital and Amobarbital (also known as Tuinal) and possession of a controlled dangerous substance, Diazepam or Valium.

Within days, officials had amassed enough evidence to charge him with the murder of Valerie Ann Street.

Eventually, after Karen Schilt and Susan Geiger identified him in a police lineup, a grand jury indicted him on charges that included two more murders, the attempted murder of another women, and the kidnapping of three others.

He continued to maintain his innocence, and October 5, 1980, through a second attorney, Peter Doyne, he entered a plea of not guilty in front of Superior Court Judge Fred C. Galda.

Cottingham was bound over for trial and held on a $350,000 bond.

The news was met with the first of three unsuccessful suicide attempts. This time, he smashed one of the lenses of his glasses and used a shard to slash his wrists. Not only did his attempt to take his own life fail, he was left without glasses for several weeks and was unable to keep up with the news articles that likely dominated more than a few front pages.

The Bergen County Record, the New York Times and the New York Daily News especially covered the Cottingham case, often with sensational front-page spreads.

"As we covered this, The Record was interested, as he was a local guy, so he was given a considerable amount of space," said Leith, who attempted to get a one-on-one interview with Cottingham, but was rebuffed.

Cottingham was all the buzz at Blue Cross Blue Shield

At work, conversations about Cottingham definitely dominated.

His coworkers were both horrified and fascinated as they learned more and more grisly details about the man they'd worked with for years.

"He was a computer main frame console operator, and I was a programmer. He was a quiet, nervous man, but he didn't give off any other signs," said one coworker after Cottingham's arrest. "He was a family man living in Lodi and no one suspected him of what he was doing. Even his wife did not know what he was doing. He gave off no signs. He had a bunch of buddies working in the computer room with him that he hung out with. They did not even know."

But then again, they did think he was a bit weird, especially Volpe, who worked so closely with Cottingham.

"I heard one time that he had a venereal disease that he contracted from a prostitute," said Volpe, "and at that point he was kind of angry when he mentioned the hooker."

Another coworker, Bruce Huff, also talked about the prostitutes Cottingham liked and the large wads of cash he would use to entice them.

Huff also mentioned Cottingham's use of "black beauties," or sedatives he would put in the glasses of prostitutes that weren't drinking enough, just as a way to loosen them up for what other fun the evening had in store.

Another coworker told police about another one workplace habit Cottingham had, which didn't really endear him to his coworkers. Cottingham, the coworker said, would steal the keys to coworkers' drawers, file cabinets, and homes, a heist that gave him access to larger-ticket items such a camera, a calculator, and meal tickets, among other things.

CHAPTER 11:
Cottingham on trial

Because he had committed his deranged crimes all over the region, Cottingham faced four separate trials in separate jurisdictions.

His first, in State Superior Court in Hackensack, New Jersey, with the Honorable Judge Paul R. Huot presiding, began in May 1981, and would last four weeks.

Jurors learned the horrifying details of Cottingham's deranged desire to torture women.

Cottingham's ruse was simple. He would tell prostitutes that he'd just won a lot of money in a card game, and wanted to take them out, not just for sex but for dinner as well, his attorney said.

"He would show them the wad of money, and of course the girls were impressed," Conway said.

He would then find a way to drug them to leave them vulnerable and incapacitated, take them to the hotel, torture them, have sex with them and then torture them some more.

His victims did not always die – it was not the murder itself that satisfied Cottingham's sexual urges, but the torture. If he victims died before he had finished having his fun, he would continue to torture them until he was satisfied, both emotionally and sexually.

The testimony would be grueling for everyone involved.

He faced one charge of murder along with charges of the kidnapping, assault, and attempted murder of four other women, all of whom testified against the computer operator.

He was indicted not only for the murder of Valerie Ann Street, but also the attempted murder of Leslie O'Dell and the kidnapping and assault of prostitutes Susan Geiger and Pamela Weisenfeld and cocktail waitress Karen Schilt.

A surprising suspect

A family man with three children, Cottingham looked like everyman when he sat beside his defense attorney.

Janet had since withdrawn her divorce and stood by her husband during his four trials.

"His wife, she described him as a devoted husband, and said he was very attentive to his children," Calo said.

Neighbors said that while Cottingham was the private type, he was a devoted dad who traditionally took his three kids trick-or-treating every Halloween.

His younger sister was also convinced that the brother she'd grown up with was no serial killer.

"She was extremely upset with me because I had brought out where they lived, so the family was upset and embarrassed, adamant in his defense through the end," said Rod Leigh, who covered the trial for the Bergen County Record. "I felt sorry for his wife, and I pitied his sister who fought the obvious truth in her brother."

But Calo and his team of prosecutors – and Cottingham's own defense attorney, for that matter – knew they were looking at a monster.

For his part, Cottingham took notes throughout the entire trial, tracking every bit of evidence against him so he could look for ways to place the blame squarely on someone else.

"He was very calm and collected during the trial, a very intelligent man, very involved in his defense, and he would pass notes to his attorneys to tell them what he thought they should do," said lead prosecutor Caro.

And although he had been advised not to take the stand, the narcissist in him couldn't resist the opportunity to talk – and to attempt to pull one over on police by offering up alibis that were flimsy at best.

"I told him, 'You're going to be cross examined, and there are a lot of holes in your story that probably will be exposed,' but he wanted to testify," said Conway.

That's where Cottingham's narcissism tripped him up. He thought that he would be able to read the room and use the information he gathered to not only play those questioning him but also the jury. His mission was to win everyone over and gain their trust, the same way he had with the prostitutes and other women he lured to their deaths.

Of course this time, pockets full of cash would be of no benefit.

"A guy like Cottingham enjoys being smarter than other people, particularly law enforcement. He thinks he's the smartest person in the room no matter where he is," said Schlesinger.

Chilling since childhood

The courtroom learned a lot about Cottingham during his first four-week trial.

Cottingham told the court that he has long fantasized about tying up defenseless women and having them at his mercy.

"The whole idea of bondage had aroused and fascinated me since I was very young," Cottingham said under questioning from Conway.

He told the courtroom that he often demanded that his victims call him "master," and when they failed to do so, there were grave consequences for the helpless women.

But murder? Of course not.

During his four hours on the stand, Cottingham claimed he was at work or with his girlfriend when four of the five incidents occurred.

He denied kidnapping and assaulting Susan Geiger and Pamela Weisenfeld, both prostitutes, and denied his assault on cocktail waitress Karen Schilt, although all of them took the stand to testify against him and point him out to the rest of the court as their assailant.

He also denied the mutilation and murder of Valerie Ann Street, who was just 18 when she made the mistake of picking Cottingham as her next trick. However damning the fingerprint on the handcuffs she was wearing, one of Cottingham's thumb, the narcissist brushed it off as nothing.

As for the testimony of William J. Van Atta, a fingerprint specialist with the Federal Bureau of Investigation, who testified that the thumbprint was definitely Cottingham's and demonstrated how it was made for the jury, well, Cottingham likely hoped the pool of his peers would completely forget.

He also hoped that they were able to overlook the similarities between the assaults, especially so the savagely bitten nipples that were in essence Cottingham's callous calling card.

The timeline of Valerie Ann Street's death

One of the main bits of evidence offered by the prosecution was the time of Valerie Ann Street's death, and how easy it would have been for Cottingham to fit it into his 3 to 11 p.m. work schedule.

According to Dr. Louis V. Napolitano, Valerie Ann was killed between 9:30 a.m. and 5:30 p.m. on May 4, 1980, a length of time that could now be significantly more narrowed given the new technology detectives and medical examiners use to determine times of death decades later.

Cottingham's wife, Janet, and his uncle, John Choromanski, both said that Cottingham was at home in Lodi from 5 a.m. to 1:30 p.m. He arrived at work at Blue Cross Blue Shield at about 3:45 p.m., according to his John Forgione.

That left a period of about two and a half hours that was unaccounted for. Was it enough time to torture a woman to his satisfaction, given the devious, detailed approach he used, first making small cuts, and then stabbing as the sight of blood and his arousal made him more frenzied? Was it enough time to rape and sodomize Valerie and then stuff her body beneath the mattress? Was it enough time to clean up?

It's seems unlikely, given Cottingham's lust for extended torture sessions that caused as much pain and fear as possible.

But more likely, the people who knew Cottingham and didn't believe that he could possibly be a serial killer were lying to protect him.

Girlfriend talks

Not everyone in Cottingham's circle felt compelled to protect him, however.

Barbara Lucas, Cottingham's girlfriend, said she's been to the Quality Inn twice with Cottingham, who clearly had no concerns about being noticed by hotel staff.

He was driving a green Ford Thunderbird, Lucas said.

Susan Geiger, although she remembered little else from the night she was savagely assaulted by Cottingham, remembered the car, a dirty Ford Thunderbird. And she remembered the color. It was green.

Survivors' testimony leaves courtroom reeling

The testimony of his surviving victims was so horrifying that it would not matter much if even some choice bits of evidence were wiped from the jury's memory.

Leslie O'Dell said that Cottingham picked her up on the corner of Lexington Avenue and 25th Street during the early hours of

May 22, 1980, and they agreed that he would pay her $100 for sex, a number that doesn't match Cottingham's price of $180.

They stopped at first a bar and then a diner before he took her to the Quality Inn in Hasbrouck Heights, the same hotel where the bodies of Valerie Ann Street and Mary Ann Car were found. They arrived sometime before dawn.

In the hours that followed, Leslie O'Dell was handcuffed, cut with a knife, bitten, and warned of the terrible fate that awaited her.

Cottingham raped her repeatedly, sodomized her, and forced her to give him oral sex, each act more violent and reprehensible than the last.

Made even worse for Leslie was that she was the only one of Cottingham's surviving victims who was not drugged, so she was aware of every horrific minute — aside from the times she nearly blacked out. But then, Cottingham used cool water to bring her back around so he could resume his fun and games.

Cottingham continued to deny any involvement in the abductions and tortures of the three women who had already testified, and as for his encounter with Leslie, he continued to say that the bloody, pain-fused sexual encounter was completely consensual.

O'Dell was grateful she escaped with her life.

"He told me to shut up, that I was a whore and I had to be punished," said O'Dell, a native of Olympia, Washington, who crossed from coast to coast in search of a dream. "'He said the other girls took it and I had to take it, too. He said that uncountable times."

Soon enough, she would be screaming for her life, and gratefully snapping back to reality when the "Do Not Disturb" sign was tossed aside, hotel staff opened the door, and she saw sweet freedom in the carpeted hall on the other side of the door.

Prosecution takes on psychopath

Bergen County's tough prosecutor, sizing up his stack of evidence, took every opportunity to trip up his suspect.

"I didn't like Mr. Cottingham, and I wanted him to know that I was out to get him," said Caro, who did his best to throw the defendant off his game. "I wanted to convict him. I wanted to put him away for the rest of his life."

He also wanted to prove that he and the police who played a role in apprehending Cottingham were smarter by far than the narcissistic, sadistic man dressing in orange and shackled in chains in the courtroom.

"Mr. Cottingham was a very intelligent man. But he was not as intelligent as he thought he was," Caro said. "He thought he was more intelligent than everybody else. That was part of his personality. But he could not deny that he was arrested with multiple pairs of handcuffs, and that handcuffs were used in the murders of Mary Ann Carr and Valerie Ann Street. He could not deny that he had gags. He could not deny that he had a knife. He could not deny that he had barbiturates. He could not deny that he bit Leslie Ann's breasts."

His defense attorney could almost hear his client's wheels turning as they sat next to one another in the Hackensack courtroom.

"You could sense that he was calculating," said Conway. "I came to the conclusion that he was devious at best. After several weeks in court, everybody – the judge, the jury – had the same opinion."

An inside look

According to reporter Rod Leith, who covered the trial, Cottingham's lawyers used a classic trick and attempted to disparage the reputations of the surviving victims, many of them prostitutes, while they were testifying on the stand.

Conway also suggested that the crime scenes were too different, "there were variations of methodology, and the killer couldn't be the same person as there were too many variables. But the general modus operandi was the same, and when New York became too dangerous for him, he came to New Jersey, along Routes 46 and 17," Leith said.

He also attempted to show jurors that Cottingham was an ideal employee, devoted to his job.

That proved less effective, because one of Cottingham's coworkers, Alan Mackie, said Cottingham frequently would leave work early on Saturdays, although he was unable to say if the days Cottingham left before quitting time were the same days of the assaults.

There was also that evidence that Cottingham stole from his coworkers, so his character was called into significant question.

Volpe also took the stand and testified about how Cottingham used to brag about the money he used to lure prostitutes. Volpe also said that Cottingham drugged his victims' drinks before taking the incapacitated victims to New Jersey, where he felt more familiar with the territory.

All in all, the evidence on the other side was overwhelming.

"The prosecution had evidence to build a case. Jewelry was a big part of it, traced back to him, plus eyewitness accounts from motels, and items he stole from victims," Leith said.

In June of 1981, Cottingham was convicted on fifteen of the twenty-one felony counts he had originally faced.

Overwhelmed by the idea of a life behind bars, three days later, Cottingham attempted suicide in his jail cell by drinking six ounces of liquid antidepressants.

Guards were unable to awaken him after the incident, and Cottingham was transported to Hackensack Hospital where he was stabilized. For a man who thought he'd mastered the fine art of death, survival had to seem like the ultimate of failures.

The next month, on July 25, Cottingham was sentenced to 173 to 197 years in prison for the murder of Valerie Ann Street and the assaults of the four other women, including Leslie O'Dell. He was also fined $2,350, essentially pocket change for the man who'd used handfuls of cash to entice his victims.

Under the terms, he would not be eligible for parole for at least 30 years.

Cottingham goes on trial for murder of Mary Ann Carr

But Cottingham's days in a courtroom were far from over.

He still faced numerous other charges, including the murder of the woman who had lived in the same apartment complex where Cottingham and his wife started their lives together, Mary Ann Carr.

Three days into his trial for that murder, on February 25, 1982, Cottingham collapsed in an elevator while being escorted back to his jail cell after the day's deliberations, which focused primarily on jury selection.

Cottingham was rushed to Bergen Pines County Hospital in Paramus, New Jersey, where he was diagnosed with a duodenal ulcer, and a mistrial was declared.

Frank Wagner, Cottingham's court-appointed defense attorney, requested the mistrial because his client would be unable to attend court proceedings due to his illness, as he was expected to be hospitalized for at least three to four days.

Bergen County Superior Court Judge James F. Madden granted the motion for a retrial and excused the thirteen prospective jurors chosen during the first three days of the trial, telling them it would be unfair to hold them indefinitely waiting for Cottingham to be healthy enough to return to trial.

When Cottingham was stabilized, he was transferred to the hospital unit at Trenton State Prison.

No date was immediately set for a retrial.

Mary Ann Carr trial beings again

On September 28, 1982, Richard Cottingham again went on trial for the murder of X-ray technician Mary Ann Carr, the pretty brunette who was just starting her married life at Little Ferry's Ledgeview Terrace apartment complex.

This time, Cottingham requested a non-jury trial, still insisting he was not guilty. He chose instead to hedge his bets on the opinion of one man, Bergen County Superior Court Judge Fred C. Galda.

Evidence, again presented by Bergen County District Attorney Dennis Calo, who had already secured a life sentence for Cottingham, included traces of white adhesive tape that Cottingham had used as a gag to silence Mary Ann.

It was the same type of tape that Cottingham had been carrying in his pocket when he was arrested after the brutal assault on Leslie O'Dell.

Even more telling, the method of the murder of Mary Ann Carr was almost a mirror image of that of Valerie Ann Street, who was found handcuffed, mutilated, and murdered in the same motel where Cottingham had abandoned Mary Ann's body like so much trash. Both bodies had handcuff marks on their hands and ankles as well as ligature marks left behind from strangulation. Valerie Ann also had the same tape residue across her mouth.

When the fake names he'd written in hotel registries were analyzed against his penmanship on items found at his home, they were a match.

And the souvenirs that were found in his trophy room sealed the deal.

The evidence was a prosecutor's dream, and Cottingham apparently knew it.

Curses, escape attempt foiled again

About a week into his trial, Cottingham must not have been feeling as certain he could manipulate the judge as he was when he made the decision to skip the jury trial and let one person decide his fate.

On October 3, 1982, Cottingham somehow managed to escape from the holding cell during lunch and made it all the way out of the courthouse, which likely gave him a sweet glimpse of freedom, something he rarely afforded any of his victims.

Officer Alan Grieco spotted the defendant as he was coming back to the courthouse after grabbing a bite to eat.

"I could see him running from the courthouse across the street," said Grieco. "Another sheriff's officer had spotted him as well, and we both tackled him on the street and put him in handcuffs and restrained him and brought him back to the courthouse."

On October 13, 1982, after just over two weeks of testimony, Cottingham was found guilty of the murder of Mary Ann Carr by Judge Galda.

In rendering his decision, Galda said that the evidence presented "clearly and convincingly satisfied this court ... that the modus operandi in respect to these cases are so unique and novel ... that it had to be the handiwork of Richard Cottingham in this case."

Mary Ann Carr's mother was overwhelmed and screamed, "My God, thank God," after the verdict was delivered.

Wagner said he would appeal the verdict, but it wouldn't matter much in terms of Cottingham's future.

On October 15, Cottingham was sentenced to 25 years to life for taking the life of Mary Ann Carr, with a minimum of 30 years to be served consecutively with his previous sentence.

CHAPTER 12:
New York trial

On March 30, 1983, Cottingham was transferred from the maximum security state prison in Trenton to the men's house of detention in Manhattan, nicknamed the Tombs, to go on trial for the murders of Deedeh Goodarzi, the Jane Doe who was also in Goodarzi's hotel room tomb, and Jean Reyner.

On July 5, 1984, a few days before the New York verdict, Cottingham again attempted suicide by cutting his left forearm with a razor, this time in front of the jury. Again, he failed to successfully take his own life.

Four days later, an unsympathetic jury of seven men and five women deliberated less than three hours before they found Cottingham guilty of the August 1980 charges of murdering the three women.

On August 28, 1984, he was sentenced to an addition 75 years to life in prison.

"I want to make sure he never kills anyone again," said Justice Sybil Hart Kooper when handing down the maximum sentence

Cottingham could have faced for the mutilation, murder, and torching of his three helpless victims.

After the sentencing, Cottingham was moved back to New Jersey, where he would finish out his sentence at Trenton State Prison, now known as New Jersey State Prison, a maximum security facility that's not only the oldest detention facility in New Jersey, but also one of the oldest in the United States.

He is housed among inmates including Jesse Timmendequas, who was sentenced to death for the rape and murder of 7-year-old Megan Kanka, the crime that led to the passage of Megan's Law, which requires neighborhoods to be notified when a convicted sex offender moves nearby.

The prison was also once home to Bruno Hauptmann, a household name in the 1930s for the kidnapping and murder of famed aviator Charles Lindbergh's toddler son.

CHAPTER 13:
Cottingham confesses to first murder, solving cold case

It was in 2010 when Cottingham gave New Jersey police a present of sorts — a confession to the murder of yet another woman, closing a case that had been cold since 1967.

Nancy Schiava Vogel was killed long before Richard Cottingham was on anybody's radar, before he had fully established his calling card, and her death had been one of the oldest cold cases in Bergen County.

Eventually however, Cottingham had a moment when his psychotic, narcissistic veneer slipped off, and he quietly confessed his crime to police.

He pled guilty to his first murder in front of Bergen County Superior Court Judge Donald R. Venezia on August 25 in Hackensack, New Jersey, and surprisingly, offered an apology for his actions to Vogel's brother and her two children, who were in the courtroom.

It was the first time he'd acknowledged any sort of responsibility for any of his crimes.

Nonetheless, he was sentenced to another life sentence, this one to also run concurrent with his existing sentences. For Cottingham, death in prison will be his end.

"Obviously, I must be sick somehow," he said. "Normal people don't do what I did."

Detectives and other law enforcement officials had been working him for a long time, and the confession was, Molinelli said in a newspaper interview, "the culmination of years of traveling to the prison" to get the madman to talk.

"After a thorough investigation and after speaking to Mr. Cottingham, we are, and were, clearly satisfied that he was the person responsible for the murder," Molinelli said.

Other cold cases could have been Cottingham

While reporters questioned whether or not Cottingham could be responsible for other cold cases, police said at the time that he was not linked to any others.

"We always look at many past defendants for possible connections with all cases, but we have nothing active at this time," Molinelli said.

Cottingham's attorney in this case, James P. Kimball, said, "I don't know if there would be any further discussions that will happen. Whether or not either side wishes to engage, we'll have to wait and see."

At the time, Bergen County had six unsolved murders, including the August 1974 murders of 17-year-old Maryann Pryor and her 16-year-old friend Lorraine Kelly, who disappeared while on a shopping trip to Paramus.

The girls were both raped and beaten, and both their wrists and ankles had been bound. Their bodies were disposed of in Montvale, the same place Cottingham killed Nancy Vogel. Given his bold declaration that he had killed many more victims that he'd ever been charged with murdering, it would come as no surprise that the two girls were among his victims, despite an intense investigation at the time of Cottingham's arrest looking into that possibility.

It's also possible that teenage hooker Helen Sikes, who disappeared from Times Square in January of 1979, could have been one of Cottingham's victims, although it has never been proven. Her body was found in Queens, her throat slashed so deeply that her head was nearly decapitated. It was her legs, however, that made investigators take a close look at Richard Cottingham. Those were found a block away from the rest of Sikes' body, positioned side by side as though they were still attached to her body.

CHAPTER 14:
The Aftermath

Now that he's safely behind bars, no one else will ever fall prey to Cottingham's cruel desires.

But for those who did – 28-year-old Mary Ann Carr, 23-year-old Deedeh Goodarzi and the teenage Jane Doe who was with her and will likely never be identified, 19-year-old Valerie Ann Street, 25-year-old Jean Reyner, and 29-year-old mom of two Nancy Vogel, along with survivors Karen Schilt, Susan Geiger, and Leslie Ann O'Dell, who brought an end to the sadistic violence – the universe had shifted.

Families would never recover from the pain of losing their child, sibling or spouse, and victims would always be haunted by the memories of their torture, especially so when they looked at the scars left behind from their ordeals.

Two books are born

Reporter Rod Leith, who covered Cottingham at length before, during and after the trial, wrote two books, "The Torso Killer" and "The Prostitute Murders," about his experiences covering the assaults and murders, the hunt for the suspect, and the subsequent trials.

"I never had encountered this kind of dark evil in any of the subjects I covered. I had written about some deeply disturbed people, but not anyone who was as treacherous and deviant as Cottingham," Leith said. "I found it to be fascinating and challenging. He was a con artist and a psychopath who lived a double life."

Leith spent five years at the Daily Record in Morristown before joining the staff at the Bergen County Record, just before Richard Cottingham began his second wave of sadistic murder, 10 years after the murder of Nancy Vogel.

While Leith's first beat was mental health, he eventually moved to organized crime, so taking on the Cottingham case was no big stretch for the seasoned reporter.

He almost immediately found himself immersed in the world that was Richard Cottingham's.

"I went to as many scenes as I could, hotels, motels, restaurants, and bars where he had been," he said, adding that the prostitutes he interviewed were terrified that they would end up the next victim. "Police never found the heads. But they knew he normally went to hotels."

Leith became almost as immersed in the sordid underbelly of Cottingham's world as police, and his investigative work led to a change in career path for the former crime reporter.

"During those years, I learned about courthouse procedures and forensic police investigations - an area of law enforcement before DNA evidence was around," he said.

Armed with those tools, he founded Rod Leith Investigations LLC, based out of Rutherford, New Jersey. The firm focuses on business intelligence and due diligence services for both corporate and individual clients.

"My reporting days taught me a great deal about people and human nature. It helped tremendously in the investigative work I've done," Leith said.

Sitting down with danger

Canadian journalist Nadia Fezzani, she herself the victim of a violent crime as a teen, spoke to Cottingham at New Jersey State Prison in Trenton, New Jersey, on February 25, 2013, in hopes of understanding why he would have committed such reprehensible acts.

"I don't comprehend how anyone could enjoy doing these things to other people, so I want to understand why," she said in a documentary that featured a portion of the interview.

It took two years for her to negotiate her visit with Cottingham and to talk the man serving a life sentence into sharing his story.

During that time, the two exchanged letters, fifteen in all, including one letter wishing Fezzani a happy birthday. He signed them all Ritchie, but was nervous about writing, because he knew investigators would want the letters, especially if he said too much.

In his first letter to her, he wrote: "I usually refuse interview requests. In fact, on the day I received your letter, '20/20' asked me for an interview. I did not even respond to them. I have turned down many lucrative proposals, for two reasons. First, I have always kept my life secret. Second, I have three children I have sworn to protect. I can only do that by remaining silent."

As she relays in her book, "Through the Eyes of Serial Killers: Interviews with Seven Murderers," Cottingham said he didn't really know why he responded to Fezzani's letter in the first place, but as an outsider looking in, the answer is quite obvious. Fezzani is pretty with long, dark hair. She was just the type that would have attracted Cottingham's attention while he was on the hunt, and clearly, his tastes hadn't changed, even after years behind bars.

She used it as an opportunity to get as much information as possible from Cottingham.

"I didn't let up. The more time that passed, the more I was driven to make him talk," she wrote.

As a way to establish a sense of trust, Cottingham asked Fezzani numerous questions about herself, including some she found embarrassing.

"He said he wanted to know more about me. It was an exchange. If he was to confide in me, I would have to do the same. I was afraid he would ask me some very personal questions, but he did not. The few times he did try, I was able to evade the question or give a vague answer," she wrote.

A fascination with danger

Fezzani had researched her serial killers well. In addition to correspondence with Cottingham, she was also exchanging letters with Joel Rifkin, Patrick Kearney, and other serial killers, trying to get into the minds of some of the worst men to ever set foot on American soil.

And there are many. Fezzani said that every year in the United States, between 50 to 100 serial killers are busy at work, taking the lives of approximately 400 victims annually. Many, such as runaways or prostitutes or hitchhikers, are never identified.

It's fascinating fodder, and in the letters he exchanged with Fezzani, Cottingham hinted that there was much more to his story than the media or the police knew, but he never delved into any details.

Face to face with a madman

Before the Cottingham interview, the experienced reporter was a bit edgy, knowing she would be sitting down with a man with the past of a barbarian.

"I'm usually not nervous like this, but if he's never spoken to the media like this, I'm really scared. He could get angry by one of the questions, he could get aggressive, or want to leave," she said.

But the two had a history, and Cottingham was happy to share his story with his longtime pen pal, especially so if he would have a chance to talk about himself.

Like Santa, but with a sadistic side

Once the two were sitting down, Cottingham with a white beard that made him look for all the world like Santa Claus, Fezzani immediately got down to business, and asked Cottingham to estimate how many women he had killed.

Cottingham was pleased but still slightly evasive about the question.

"I won't give an exact figure, but I will say this. I'm in jail for five murders, but I started to do this kind of thing twelve years before, so you do the math. Or to put it another way, the figure is higher than your age."

Times Square was Cottingham's hunting ground of choice. At the time, prostitution was prolific, so he never had any trouble picking up hookers to take to hotels and torture until he was sexually satisfied.

As to why that sexual satisfaction required the agony he'd inflicted on his victims, his answer was equally coy.

"I wanted to create a sensationalism," he said.

He told Fezzani that he cut off some victims' hands and heads with a hacksaw not only to hide their identities, but also to draw attention to his crime by putting a personalized stamp on the crime scene.

And as for the time he sliced off a prostitute's breasts in the hotel room, leaving them on the headboard like macabre décor, it was "to do something different."

He was able to do something so evil so easily, because "it's not a person anymore," he said. "It's a body. You don't feel anything."

In other words, the narcissist – like virtually every killer that takes multiple lives in deranged, twisted ways – wanted to be famous for his highly individualized crimes, which were truly as sick as they come.

"I wanted to be the best at whatever I did and I wanted to be the best serial killer. Yes.

"Even as a child I had to be the best at whatever I did, or I wouldn't do it. Subliminally, I was a manipulative control freak. It was my way or the highway."

But what remained then was the reason why.

Cottingham doesn't wonder 'why me'

According to Fezzani in her book, police called Cottingham "the enigma," because his childhood didn't seem to contain an obvious incident, molestation or severe abuse for example, that would have triggered the man's rage.

Cottingham was a good kid in school, and during his earliest years, he was well liked among his peers.

A move to a new school, however, led him to be ostracized by the other students in his class, and the rejection stung mightily.

While most serial killers require something much more serious to send them off the rails, Cottingham was a psychopath, so the smallest slight was enough to trigger a desire for revenge.

After that, he kept to himself, and he turned his rage inward, taking all the pain he felt over being rejected by his peers and using it to forge diabolical plans.

Still, he was initially unwilling to admit just what triggered his prurient desires and compared his future bad behavior to a love of living on the edge.

"I don't think there's been any one event," he said. "It's just how I grew up. I mean everything just evolved into what happened. I'm the type of person who liked to take a lot of challenges. Like I said, I'm a gambler, and I've always been a gambler. It's in my blood. And any kind of risk-taking, anything to defy the norm, I will try, I would do. And that led to one thing on and on, until I started getting brazen. But there was no specific episode or anything like that. Never got in any trouble as a kid. Never. I was an anonymous-type person, a loner. And I'm the type that has to win all the time to come out on top no matter what I'm doing. I tried to be the best at it."

And as far as the prostitutes and other women who were unfortunate enough to encounter Richard Cottingham, well, that was really more their faults than his, he said.

"A lot of them were just at the wrong place at the wrong time," he told Nadia Fezzani in the jailhouse interview. "If I would have went down a different block, or if I wouldn't have gone out that night, or if I didn't go into that particular bar, it wouldn't have happened."

But as it was, he did go out, he did visit Times Square, he did like to go out for drinks after work, and he did pick up prostitutes, many of whom died after hours of brutal suffering.

And that was all on Cottingham.

With only a few signature calling cards – the biting of the nipples, the cigarette burns, the handcuffs, the escalating mutilation of the bodies – he was fast becoming one of the most notorious, and had all of the prostitutes working Times Square totally on edge.

"Some of the prostitutes were completely frozen with fear over this guy. One woman wondered whether he was trying to make a Frankenstein whore," said Rod Leith.

Cottingham, like so many serial killers before and after him, didn't see his victims as fellow human beings and instead viewed them as toys, playthings that were there solely for his pleasure.

"I've probably done everything a man would want to do with a woman," said Cottingham, who clearly has some trouble understanding the basics of human relationships, or what real men want from their relationships with women.

Communal with madness a way to solve unanswered questions

For Nadia, the talk was painful and sometimes left her questioning why she continued to pursue serial killers and their stories.

"Sometimes I want to stop, and then my friends encourage me to go on," she said, "I think about the families and their suffering and the innocent victims. Like Cottingham, for example. I know I am the only one that he talks to, so I feel like I'm the only one who can help the victim's families. He's spoken to me about crimes he's never confessed to, and that's my victory."

While he talked about his murders, blithely and casually as if he was counting how many eggs he'd eaten for breakfast that morning, the room likely turned chilly for Nadia as she understood that the man sitting across from her, despite his jovial look, had no emotion that suggested compassion or sympathy for his victims.

And he was evasive when she asked again how many people he had killed over the years.

"Oh, I know exactly how many," he told her, chuckling to himself. "Over 85. Under 100."

His voice sounded proud as he spoke, although there was a twinge of disappointment, as if he'd wished he'd have reached a nice round even number of kills, until fate – and officers – intervened.

"I was doing this for years. Hardly a week or two went by without something happening," he said.

Cottingham was, however, despite his psychotic nature, able to establish relationships that allowed him to see others as human beings, and when Nadia asked him, "Richard, would you be able to kill me?" his answer was immediate.

"No," he said, even though there was much about Fezzani that fit his victim profile.

She asked him a second question: "Why not?"

"Because I like you," Cottingham said. "You're tough. You don't take no crap. I respect you. You would be the type I would have as a girlfriend. At least on my end. I don't know about you."

Most likely, her answer would be no, although she did visit the house Cottingham was living in during the bulk of his murders, two two-story duplex with a two-car garage and the basement with the locked room.

The surprised family that was living there had no idea about the depraved mind that had once occupied their space, and they were a bit startled by the news.

While there, Caro and Fezzani looked over photographs of Cottingham as a family man, including one with his firstborn son on the day of his baptism.

"It's strange to see that he had a human family side, that he took care of his children," Fezzani said.

Caro talked about the trial and the madness of having to show crime scene photographs to the families of victims who had suffered unimaginable torture at the hands of Cottingham, including one of Valerie Ann Street that he showed her horrified sister.

"These people's lives were just ruined," Caro said. "I showed her the photograph, and asked her if she recognized the girl in that photograph and she just broke down in sobs and said 'my sister.'"

The memory caused Caro to also tear up, and Fezzani's tears soon followed, imaging the horror of seeing one's sister, someone you'd grown up with, played with, gone to school with, gotten in to trouble with and loved deeply, mutilated and in handcuffs, dead at the hands of a man too cowardly to admit his guilt.

As for the people left behind in the aftermath of it all, they had trouble understanding how the man they knew could have been such a monster.

Question of 'why' will never have answers

"What makes them think they're going to get away with it? That's what I dwell on more than anything else," said his childhood friend, Richard Neumann. "What makes them think they can continue to do it and have this smug attitude and excise this awful power over people? There are lots of things inside our mentality that tell us not to do it, if only that that's a fellow human being, and they have loved ones at home."

But that's the thing about psychopaths.

There is no thought about another person's place in the world, or the damage that spreads like rings on water when a rock is tossed over a bridge.

"Those who are psychopathic absolutely have no remorse for what they are doing," said Ramsland. "They don't really care about people being in pain, unless they're a sadist, then they care because they want them to be in pain. A psychopath and a sadist are not one in the same, but if you get the two in combination, you have a very, very dangerous person."

Richard Cottingham was very dangerous indeed.

"He was far different from people that I've met and I've met some people from all kinds of bad backgrounds or bad situations, but he I think he's intrinsically evil," said his defense attorney Donald Conway, long after Cottingham was safely secured behind bars.

Added his former coworker, Dominick Volpe: "He fooled around with hookers, a lot of people do that. Nobody kills people. Nobody decapitates people. Nobody rips people's hands off. I think he's a sick son of a bitch."

The main book has ended, but keep turning the pages and you will find some more information as well as some free content that I've added for you!

Including one of my best-selling books!

Keep turning the pages!

GET ONE OF MY AUDIOBOOKS FOR FREE

audible
an amazon company

If you haven't joined Audible yet, you can get any of my audiobooks for FREE!

Go to www.JackRosewood.com to find out more!

More books by Jack Rosewood

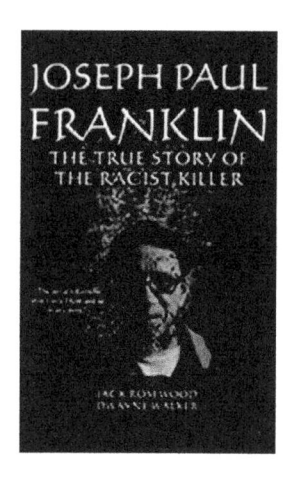

Among the annals of American serial killers, few were as complex and prolific as Joseph Paul Franklin. At a gangly 5'11, Franklin hardly looked imposing, but once he put a rifle in his hands and an interracial couple in his cross hairs, Joseph Paul Franklin was as deadly as any serial killer. In this true crime story you will learn about how one man turned his hatred into a vocation of murder, which eventually left over twenty people dead across America. Truly, Franklin's story is not only that of a true crime serial killer, but also one of racism in America as he chose Jews, blacks, and especially interracial couples as his victims.

Joseph Paul Franklin's story is unique among serial killers biographies because he gained no sexual satisfaction from his murders and there is no indication that he was ever compelled to kill. But make no mistake about it, by all definitions; Joseph Paul Franklin was a serial killer. In fact, the FBI stated that Franklin was the first known racially motivated serial killer in the United States: he planned to kill as many of his perceived enemies as possible in order to start an epic race war across the country. An examination of Franklin's life will reveal how he became a racially motivated serial killer and the steps he took to carry out his one man war against the world.

Open the pages of this e-book to read a disturbing story of true crime murder in America's heartland. You will be disturbed and perplexed at Franklin's murderous campaign as he made himself a one man death squad, eliminating as many of his political enemies that he could. But you will also be captivated with Franklin's shrewdness and cunning as he avoided the authorities for years while he carried out his diabolical plot!

The world can be a very strange place in general and when you open the pages of this true crime anthology you will quickly learn that the criminal world specifically can be as bizarre as it is dangerous. In the following book, you will be captivated by mysterious missing person cases that defy all logic and a couple cases of murderous mistaken identity. Follow along as detectives conduct criminal investigations in order to solve cases that were once believed to be unsolvable. Every one of the crime cases chronicled in the pages of this book are as strange and disturbing as the next.

The twelve true crime stories in this book will keep you riveted as you turn the pages, but they will probably also leave you with more questions than answers. For instance, you will be left pondering how two brothers from the same family could disappear with no trace in similar circumstances over ten years apart. You will also wonder how two women with the same first and last names, but with no personal connections, could be murdered within the same week in the same city. The examination of a number of true crime murder cases that went cold, but were later solved through scientific advances, will also keep you intrigued and reading.

Open the pages of this book, if you dare, to read some of the most bizarre cases of disappearances, mistaken identity, and true murder. Some of the cases will disturb and anger you, but make no mistake, you will want to keep reading!

GET THESE BOOKS FOR FREE

Go to www.jackrosewood.com
and get these E-Books for free!

A Note From The Author

Hello, this is Jack Rosewood. Thank you for reading this true crime story. I hope you enjoyed the read of this chilling story. If you did, I'd appreciate if you would take a few moments to post a review on Amazon.

I would also love if you'd sign up to my newsletter to receive updates on new releases, promotions and a FREE copy of my Herbert Mullin E-Book, go to www.JackRosewood.com

Thanks again for reading this book, make sure to follow me on Facebook.

Best Regards

Jack Rosewood

FREE BONUS CHAPTER

The making of a serial killer

"I was born with the devil in me," said H.H. Holmes, who in 1893 took advantage of the World's Fair – and the extra room he rented out in his Chicago mansion – to kill at least 27 people without attracting much attention.

"I could not help the fact that I was a murderer, no more than the poet can help the inspiration to sing. I was born with the evil one standing as my sponsor beside the bed where I was ushered into the world, and he has been with me since," Holmes said.

The idea of "I can't help it" is one of the hallmarks of many serial killers, along with an unwillingness to accept responsibility for their actions and a refusal to acknowledge that they themselves used free will to do their dreadful deeds.

"Yes, I did it, but I'm a sick man and can't be judged by the standards of other men," said Juan Corona, who killed 25 migrant workers in California in the late 1960s and early 1970s, burying them in the very fruit orchards where they'd hoped to build a better life for their families.

Dennis Rader, who called himself the BTK Killer (Bind, Torture, Kill) also blamed some unknown facet to his personality, something he called Factor X, for his casual ability to kill one family, then go home to his own, where he was a devoted family man.

"When this monster entered my brain, I will never know, but it is here to stay. How does one cure himself? I can't stop it, the monster goes on, and hurts me as well as society. Maybe you can stop him. I can't," said Rader, who said he realized he was different than the other kids before he entered high school. "I actually think I may be possessed with demons."

But again, he blamed others for not stopping him from making his first murderous move.

"You know, at some point in time, someone should have picked something up from me and identified it," he later said.

Rader was not the only serial killer to place the blame far away from himself.

William Bonin actually took offense when a judge called him "sadistic and guilty of monstrous criminal conduct."

"I don't think he had any right to say that to me," Bonin later whined. "I couldn't help myself. It's not my fault I killed those boys."

It leaves us always asking why

For those of us who are not serial killers, the questions of why and how almost always come to mind, so ill equipped are we to understand the concept of murder on such a vast scale.

"Some nights I'd lie awake asking myself, 'Who the hell is this BTK?'" said FBI profiler John Douglas, who worked the Behavioral Science Unit at Quantico before writing several best-selling books, including "Mindhunter: Inside the FBI's Elite Serial Crime Unit," and "Obsession: The FBI's Legendary Profiler Probes the Psyches of Killers, Rapists, and Stalkers and Their Victims and Tells How to Fight Back."

The questions were never far from his mind - "What makes a guy like this do what he does? What makes him tick?" – and it's the kind of thing that keeps profilers and police up at night, worrying, wondering and waiting for answers that are not always so easily forthcoming.

Another leader into the study of madmen, the late FBI profiler Robert Ressler - who coined the terms serial killer as well as criminal profiling – also spent sleepless nights trying to piece together a portrait of many a killer, something that psychiatrist James Brussel did almost unfailingly well in 1940, when a pipe bomb killer enraged at Con Edison was terrorizing New York City.

(Brussel told police what the killer would be wearing when they arrested him, and although he was caught at home late at night, wearing his pajamas, when police asked him to dress, he emerged from his room wearing a double-breasted suit, exactly as Brussel had predicted.)

"What is this force that takes a hold of a person and pushes them over the edge?" wondered Ressler, who interviewed scores of killers over the course of his illustrious career.

In an effort to infiltrate the minds of serial killers, Douglas and Ressler embarked on a mission to interview some of the most deranged serial killers in the country, starting their journey in California, which "has always had more than its share of weird and spectacular crimes," Douglas said.

In their search for a pattern, they determined that there are essential two types of serial killers: organized and disorganized.

Organized killers

Organized killers were revealed through their crime scenes, which were neat, controlled and meticulous, with effort taken both in the crime and with their victims. Organized killers also take care to leave behind few clues once they're done.

Dean Corll was an organized serial killer. He tortured his victims overnight, carefully collecting blood and bodily fluids on a sheet of plastic before rolling them up and burying them and their possessions, most beneath the floor of a boat shed he'd rented, going there late at night under the cover of darkness.

Disorganized killers

On the flip side of the coin, disorganized killers grab their victims indiscriminately, or act on the spur of the moment, allowing victims to collect evidence beneath their fingernails when they fight back and oftentimes leaving behind numerous clues including weapons.

"The disorganized killer has no idea of, or interest in, the personalities of his victims," Ressler wrote in his book "Whoever Fights Monsters," one of several detailing his work as a criminal profiler. "He does not want to know who they are, and many times takes steps to obliterate their personalities by quickly knocking them unconscious or covering their faces or otherwise disfiguring them."

Cary Stayner – also known as the Yosemite Killer – became a disorganized killer during his last murder, which occurred on the fly when he was unable to resist a pretty park educator.

Lucky for other young women in the picturesque park, he left behind a wide range of clues, including four unmatched tire tracks from his aging 1979 International Scout.

"The crime scene is presumed to reflect the murderer's behavior and personality in much the same way as furnishings reveal the homeowner's character," Douglas and Ressler later wrote, expanding on their findings as they continued their interview sessions.

Serial killers think they're unique – but they're not

Dr. Helen Morrison – a longtime fixture in the study of serial killers who keeps clown killer John Wayne Gacy's brain in her basement (after Gacy's execution she sent the brain away for an analysis that proved it to be completely normal) – said that at their core, most serial killers are essentially the same.

While psychologists still haven't determined the motives behind what drives serial killers to murder, there are certain characteristics they have in common, said Morrison, who has studied or interviewed scores of serial killers and wrote about her experiences in "My Life Among the Serial Killers."

Most often men, serial killers tend to be talkative hypochondriacs who develop a remorseless addiction to the brutality of murder.

Too, they are able to see their victims as inanimate objects, playthings, of you will, around simply for their amusement.

Empathy? Not on your life.

"They have no appreciation for the absolute agony and terror and fear that the victim is demonstrating," said Morrison. "They just see the object in front of them. A serial murderer has no feelings. Serial killers have no motives. They kill only to kill an object."

In doing so, they satisfy their urges, and quiet the tumultuous turmoil inside of them.

"You say to yourself, 'How could anybody do this to another human being?'" Morrison said. "Then you realize they don't see them as humans. To them, it's like pulling the wings off a fly or the legs off a daddy longlegs.... You just want to see what happens. It's the most base experiment."

Nature vs. nurture?

For many serial killers, the desire to kill is as innate at their hair or eye color, and out of control, but most experts say that childhood trauma is an experience shared by them all.

In 1990, Colin Wilson and Donald Seaman conducted a study of serial killers behind bars and found that childhood problems were the most influential factors that led serial killers down their particular path of death and destruction.

Former FBI profiler Robert Ressler – who coined the terms serial killer and criminal profiling – goes so far as to say that 100 percent of all serial killers experienced childhoods that were not filled with happy memories of camping trips or fishing on the lake.

According to Ressler, of all the serial killers he interviewed or studied, each had suffered some form of abuse as a child - either sexual, physical or emotional abuse, neglect or rejection by parents or humiliation, including instances that occurred at school.

For those who are already hovering psychologically on edge due to unfortunate genetics, such events become focal points that drive a killer to act on seemingly insane instincts.

Because there is often no solid family unit – parents are missing or more focused on drugs and alcohol, sexual abuse goes unnoticed, physical abuse is commonplace – the child's development becomes stunted, and they can either develop deep-seeded rage or create for themselves a fantasy world where everything is perfect, and they are essentially the kings of their self-made castle.

That was the world of Jeffrey Dahmer, who recognized his need for control much later, after hours spent in analysis where he learned the impact of a sexual assault as a child as well as his parents' messy, rage-filled divorce.

"After I left the home, that's when I started wanting to create my own little world, where I was the one who had complete control," Dahmer said. "I just took it way too far."

Dahmer's experiences suggest that psychopathic behavior likely develops in childhood, when due to neglect and abuse, children revert to a place of fantasy, a world where the victimization of the child shifts toward others.

"The child becomes sociopathic because the normal development of the concepts of right and wrong and empathy towards others is retarded because the child's emotional and social development occurs within his self-centered fantasies. A person can do no wrong in his own world and the pain of others is of no consequence when the purpose of the fantasy world is to satisfy the needs of one person," according to one expert.

As the lines between fantasy and reality become blurred, fantasies that on their own are harmless become real, and monsters like Dean Corll find themselves strapping young boys down to a wooden board, raping them, torturing them and listening to them scream, treating the act like little more than a dissociative art project that ends in murder.

Going inside the mind: Psychopathy and other mental illnesses

While not all psychopaths are serial killers – many compulsive killers do feel some sense of remorse, such as Green River Killer Gary Ridgeway did when he cried in court after one victim's father offered Ridgeway his forgiveness – those who are, Morrison said, are unable to feel a speck of empathy for their victims.

Their focus is entirely on themselves and the power they are able to assert over others, especially so in the case of a psychopath.

Psychopaths are charming – think Ted Bundy, who had no trouble luring young women into his car by eliciting sympathy with a faked injury – and have the skills to easily manipulate their victims, or in some cases, their accomplices.

Dean Corll was called a Svengali – a name taken from a fictional character in George du Maurier's 1895 novel "Trilby" who seduces, dominates and exploits the main character, a young girl – for being able to enlist the help of several neighborhood boys who procured his youthful male victims without remorse, even when the teens were their friends.

Some specific traits of serial killers, determined through years of profiling, include:

- **Smooth talking but insincere.** Ted Bundy was a charmer, the kind of guy that made it easy for people to be swept into his web. "I liked him immediately, but people like Ted can fool you completely," said Ann Rule, author of the best-selling "Stranger Beside Me," about her experiences with Bundy, a man she considered a friend. "I'd been a cop, had all that psychology — but his mask was perfect. I say that long acquaintance can help you know someone. But you can never be really sure. Scary."
- **Egocentric and grandiose.** Jack the Ripper thought the world of himself, and felt he would outsmart police, so much so that he sent letters taunting the London

officers. "Dear Boss," he wrote, "I keep on hearing the police have caught me but they won't fix me just yet. I have laughed when they look so clever and talk about being on the right track. That joke about Leather Apron gave me real fits. I am down on whores and I shan't quit ripping them till I do get buckled. Grand work the last job was. I gave the lady no time to squeal. How can they catch me now? I love my work and want to start again. You will soon hear of me with my funny little games. I saved some of the proper red stuff in a ginger beer bottle over the last job to write with but it went thick like glue and I can't use it. Red ink is fit enough I hope ha. ha. The next job I do I shall clip the lady's ears off and send to the police officers ... My knife's so nice and sharp I want to get to work right away if I get a chance. Good luck."

- **Lack of remorse or guilt.** Joel Rifkin was filled with self-pity after he was convicted of killing and dismembering at least nine women. He called his conviction a tragedy, but later, in prison, he got into an argument with mass murderer Colin Ferguson over whose killing spree was more important, and when Ferguson taunted him for only killing women, Rifkin said, "Yeah, but I had more victims."

- **Lack of empathy.** Andrei Chikatilo, who feasted on bits of genitalia both male and female after his kills, thought nothing of taking a life, no matter how torturous it was for his victims. "The whole thing - the cries, the blood, the agony - gave me relaxation and a certain pleasure," he said.

- **Deceitful and manipulative.** John Wayne Gacy refused to take responsibility for the 28 boys buried beneath his house, even though he also once said that clowns can get away with murder. "I think after 14 years under truth serum had I committed the crime I would have known it," said the man the neighbors all claimed to like. "There's got to be something that would... would click in my mind. I've had photos of 21 of the victims and I've looked at them all over the years here and I've never recognized anyone of them."

- **Shallow emotions.** German serial killer Rudolph Pliel, convicted of killing 10 people and later took his own life in prison, compared his "hobby" of murder to playing cards, and later told police, "What I did is not such a great harm, with all these surplus women nowadays. Anyway, I had a good time."

- **Impulsive.** Tommy Lynn Sells, who claimed responsibility for dozens of murders throughout the Midwest and South, saw a woman at a convenience store and followed her home, an impulse he was unable to control. He waited until the house went dark, then "I went into this house. I go to the first bedroom I see...I don't know whose room it is and, and, and, and I start stabbing." The victim was the woman's young son.

- **Poor behavior controls**. "I wished I could stop but I could not. I had no other thrill or happiness," said UK killer Dennis Nilsen, who killed at least 12 young men via strangulation, then bathed and dressed their bodies before disposing of them, often by burning them.
- **Need for excitement.** For Albert Fish - a masochistic killer with a side of sadism that included sending a letter to the mother of one of his victims, describing in detail how he cut, cooked and ate her daughter - even the idea of his own death was one he found particularly thrilling. "Going to the electric chair will be the supreme thrill of my life," he said.
- **Lack of responsibility.** "I see myself more as a victim rather than a perpetrator," said Gacy, in a rare moment of admitting the murders. "I was cheated out of my childhood. I should never have been convicted of anything more serious than running a cemetery without a license. They were just a bunch of worthless little queers and punks."
- **Early behavior problems.** "When I was a boy I never had a friend in the world," said German serial killer Heinrich Pommerencke, who began raping and murdering girls as a teen.

- **Adult antisocial behavior.** Gary Ridgeway pleaded guilty to killing 48 women, mostly prostitutes, who were easy prey and were rarely reported missing – at least not immediately. "I don't believe in man, God nor Devil. I hate the whole damned human race, including myself... I preyed upon the weak, the harmless and the unsuspecting. This lesson I was taught by others: Might makes right."

'I felt like it'

Many psychopaths will say after a crime, "I did it because I felt like it," with a certain element of pride.

That's how BTK killer Dennis Rader felt, and because he had no sense of wrong regarding his actions, he was able to carry on with his normal life with his wife and children with ease.

Someone else's demeanor might have changed, they may have become jittery or anxious, and they would have been caught.

Many serial killers are so cold they are can pop into a diner right after a murder, never showing a sign of what they've done.

"Serial murderers often seem normal," according to the FBI. "They have families and/or a steady job."

"They're so completely ordinary," Morrison added. "That's what gets a lot of victims in trouble."

That normalcy is often what allows perpetrators to get away with their crimes for so long.

Unlike mass murderers such as terrorists who generally drop off the radar before perpetrating their event, serial killers blend in. They might seem a bit strange – neighbors noticed that Ed Gein wasn't too big on personal hygiene, and neighbors did think it was odd that William Bonin hung out with such young boys - but not so much so that anyone would ask too many questions.

"That's why so many people often say, "I had no idea" or "He was such a nice guy" after a friend or neighbor is arrested.

And it's also why people are so very, very stunned when they see stories of serial killers dominating the news.

"For a person with a conscience, Rader's crimes seem hideous, but from his point of view, these are his greatest accomplishments and he is anxious to share all of the wonderful things he has done," said Jack Levin, PhD, director of the Brudnick Center on Violence and Conflict at Northeastern University in Boston and the author of "Extreme Killings."

A new take on psychopathy

Psychopathy is now diagnosed as antisocial personality disorder, a prettier spin on an absolutely horrifying diagnosis.

According to studies, almost 50 percent of men in prison and 21 percent of women in prison have been diagnosed with antisocial personality disorder.

Of serial killers, Ted Bundy (who enjoyed sex with his dead victims), John Wayne Gacy and Charles Manson (who encouraged others to do his dirty work which included the murder of pregnant Sharon Tate) were all diagnosed with this particular affliction, which allowed them to carry out their crimes with total disregard toward others or toward the law.

They showed no remorse.

Schizophrenia

Many known serial killers were later diagnosed with some other form of mental illness, including schizophrenia, believed to be behind the crimes of David Berkowitz (he said his neighbor's dog told him to kill his six victims in the 1970s), Ed Gein, whose grisly saving of skin, bones and various female sex parts was a desperate effort to resurrect his death mother and Richard Chase (the vampire of Sacramento, who killed six people in California in order to drink their blood).

Schizophrenia includes a wide range of symptoms, ranging from hallucinations and delusions to living in a catatonic state.

Borderline personality disorder

Borderline personality disorder – which is characterized by intense mood swings, problems with interpersonal relationships and impulsive behaviors – is also common in serial killers.

Some diagnosed cases of borderline personality disorder include Aileen Wuornos, a woman whose horrific childhood and numerous sexual assaults led her to murder one of her rapists, after which she spiraled out of control and killed six other men who picked her up along with highway in Florida, nurse Kristen H. Gilbert, who killed four patients at a Virginia hospital with overdoses of epinephrine, and Dahmer, whose murder count rose to 17 before he was caught.

With a stigma still quite present regarding mental illness, it's likely we will continue to diagnose serial killers and mass murderers after the fact, too late to protect their victims.

Top signs of a serial killer

While there is still no simple thread of similarities – which is why police and the FBI have more trouble in real life solving crimes than they do on shows like "Criminal Minds" – there are some things to look for, experts say.

- **Antisocial Behavior.** Psychopaths tend to be loners, so if a child that was once gregarious and outgoing becomes shy and antisocial, this could be an issue. Jeffrey Dahmer was a social, lively child until his parents moved to Ohio for his father's new job. There, he regressed – allegedly after being sexually molested – and began focusing his attentions on dissecting road kill rather than developing friendships.

- **Arson.** Fire is power, and power and control are part of the appeal for serial killers, who enjoy having their victims at their mercy. David Berkowitz was a pyromaniac as a child – his classmates called him Pyro as a nickname, so well-known was he for his fire obsession - and he reportedly started more than 1,000 fires in New York before he became the Son of Sam killer.

- **Torturing animals.** Serial killers often start young, and test boundaries with animals including family or neighborhood pets. According to studies, 70 percent of violent offenders have episodes of animal abuse in their childhood histories, compared to just 6 percent of nonviolent offenders. Albert DeSalvo – better known as the Boston Strangler – would capture cats and dogs as a child and trap them in boxes, shooting arrows at the defenseless animals for sport.

- **A troubled family history.** Many serial killers come from families with criminal or psychiatric histories or alcoholism. Edmund Kemper killed his grandparents to see what it would be like, and later – after he murdered a string of college students – he killed his alcoholic mother, grinding her vocal chords in the garbage disposal in an attempt to erase the sound of her voice.

- **Childhood abuse.** William Bonin – who killed at least 21 boys and young men in violent rapes and murders – was abandoned as a child, sent to live in a group home where he himself was sexually assaulted. The connections suggest either a rage that can't be erased – Aileen Wuornos, a rare female serial killer, was physically and sexually abused throughout her childhood, resulting in distrust of others and a pent-up rage that exploded during a later rape - or a disassociation of sorts, refusing to connect on a human level with others for fear of being rejected yet again.
- **Substance abuse.** Many serial killers use drugs or alcohol. Jeffrey Dahmer was discharged from the Army due to a drinking problem he developed in high school, and he used alcohol to lure his victims to his apartment, where he killed them in a fruitless effort to create a zombie-like sex slave who would never leave him.
- **Voyeurism.** When Ted Bundy was a teen, he spent his nights as a Peeping Tom, hoping to get a glimpse of one of the neighborhood girls getting undressed in their bedrooms.
- **Serial killers are usually smart.** While their IQ is not usually the reason why serial killers elude police for so long, many have very high IQs. Edmund Kemper was

thisclose to being considered a genius (his IQ was 136, just four points beneath the 140 mark that earns genius status), and he used his intelligence to create complex cons that got him released from prison early after killing his grandparents, allowing eight more women to die.

- **Can't keep a job.** Serial killers often have trouble staying employed, either because their off-hours activities take up a lot of time (Jeffrey Dahmer hid bodies in his shower, the shower he used every morning before work, because he was killing at such a fast rate) or because their obsessions have them hunting for victims when they should be on the clock.

Trademarks of a serial killer

While what we know helps us get a better understanding of potential serial killers — and perhaps take a closer look at our weird little neighbors — it is still tricky for police and FBI agents to track serial killers down without knowing a few tells.

The signature

While serial killers like to stake a claim over their killings — "Serial killers typically have some sort of a signature," according to Dr. Scott Bonn, a professor at Drew University in New Jersey — they are usually still quite neat, and a signature does not necessarily mean evidence.

"Jack the Ripper, of course, his signature was the ripping of the bodies," said Bonn.

While there are multiple theories, Jack the Ripper has yet to be identified, despite the similarities in his murders.

Too, the Happy Face Killer, Keith Hunter Jespersen – whose childhood was marked by alcoholic parents, teasing at school and a propensity to abuse small animals - drew happy faces on the numerous letters he sent to both media and authorities, teasing them a bit with a carrot on a string.

"If the forensic evidence itself - depending upon the bones or flesh or whatever is left - if it allows for that sort of identification, that would be one way of using forensic evidence to link these murders," Bonn said.

The cooling off period

Organized killers are so neat, tidy and meticulous that they may never leave clues, even if they have a signature.

And if there's a long cooling off period between crimes, tracking the killer becomes even more of a challenge.

After a murder – which could be compared to a sexual experience or getting high on drugs – the uncontrollable urges that led the killer to act dissipate, at least temporarily.

But according to Ressler, serial killers are rarely satisfied with their kills, and each one increases desire – in the same way a porn addiction can start with the pages of Playboy then turn into BDSM videos or other fetishes when Playboy pictorials are no longer satisfying.

"I was literally singing to myself on my way home, after the killing. The tension, the desire to kill a woman had built up in such explosive proportions that when I finally pulled the trigger, all the pressures, all the tensions, all the hatred, had just vanished, dissipated, but only for a short time," said David Berkowitz, better known as the Son of Sam.

Afterwards, the memory of the murder, or mementos from the murder such as the skulls Jeffrey Dahmer retained, the scalps collected by David Gore or the box of vulvas Ed Gein kept in his kitchen, no longer become enough, and the killers must kill again, creating a "serial" cycle.

That window between crimes usually becomes smaller, however, which allows authorities to notice similarities in murder scenes or methodology, making tracking easier.

In the case of William Bonin, there were months between his first few murders, but toward the end, he sometimes killed two young men a day to satisfy his increasingly uncontrollable urges.

"Sometimes... I'd get tense and think I was gonna go crazy if I couldn't get some release, like my head would explode. So I'd go out hunting. Killing helped me... It was like ... needing to go gambling or getting drunk. I had to do it," Bonin said.

Hunting in pairs

Some serial killers – between 10 and 25 percent - find working as a team more efficient, and they use their charm as the hook to lure in accomplices.

Ed Gein may never have killed anyone had his accomplice, a mentally challenged man who helped Gein dig up the graves of women who resembled his mother, not been sent to a nursing home, leaving Gein unable to dig up the dead on his own.

Texas killer Dean Corll used beer, drugs, money and candy to bribe neighborhood boys to bring him their friends for what they were promised was a party, but instead would turn to torture and murder. He would have killed many more if one of his accomplices had not finally shot him to prevent another night of death.

William Bonin also liked to work with friends, and he enticed boys who were reportedly on the low end of the IQ scale to help him sadistically rape and torture his victims.

Other red flags

According to the FBI's Behavioral Science Unit – founded by Robert Ressler - 60 percent of murderers whose crimes involved sex were childhood bed wetters, and sometimes carried the habit into adulthood. One such serial killer, Alton Coleman, regularly wet his pants, earning the humiliating nickname "Pissy."

Sexual arousal over violent fantasies during puberty can also play a role in a serial killer's future.

Jeffrey Dahmer hit puberty about the same time he was dissecting road kill, so in some way, his wires became crossed and twisted, and sex and death aroused him.

Brain damage? Maybe

While Helen Morrison's test found that John Wayne Gacy's brain was normal, and Jeffrey Dahmer's father never had the opportunity to have his son's brain studied, although both he and Jeffrey had wanted the study, there is some evidence that some serial killers have brain damage that impact their ability to exact rational control.

"Normal parents? Normal brains? I think not," said Dr. Jonathan Pincus, a neurologist and author of the book "Base Instincts: What Makes Killers Kill."

"Abusive experiences, mental illnesses and neurological deficits interplayed to produce the tragedies reported in the newspapers. The most vicious criminals have also been, overwhelmingly, people who have been grotesquely abused as children and have paranoid patterns of thinking," said Pincus in his book, adding that childhood traumas can impact the developmental anatomy and functioning of the brain.

***

So what do we know?

Serial killers can be either uber-smart or brain damaged, completely people savvy or totally awkward, high functioning and seemingly normal or unable to hold down a job.

But essentially, no matter what their back story, their modus operandi or their style, "they're evil," said criminal profiler Pat Brown.

And do we need to know anything more than that?

A Note From The Author

Hello, this is Jack Rosewood. Thank you for reading this true crime story. I hope you enjoyed the read of this chilling story. If you did, I'd appreciate if you would take a few moments to post a review on Amazon.

I would also love if you'd sign up to my newsletter to receive updates on new releases, promotions and a FREE copy of my Herbert Mullin E-Book, go to www.JackRosewood.com

Thanks again for reading this book, make sure to follow me on Facebook.

Best Regards

Jack Rosewood